DATE DUE

Mar 14'66			
Apr 2'66			
Mar 18'67			
Mar 4'59			
Nov 30 70			
GAYLORD			PRINTED IN U.S.A.

PROBLEMS IN EUROPEAN CIVILIZATION

UNDER THE EDITORIAL DIRECTION OF

Ralph W. Greenlaw* and Dwight E. Lee†

Other volumes in preparation

1848

A Turning Point?

PROBLEMS IN EUROPEAN CIVILIZATION

1848

A Turning Point?

EDITED WITH AN INTRODUCTION BY

Melvin Kranzberg

CASE INSTITUTE OF TECHNOLOGY

D. C. HEATH AND COMPANY · BOSTON

In the case of sale outside the United States, special acknowledgment is made to Hamish Hamilton Ltd. for permission to reprint the selection from A. J. P. Taylor's THE COURSE OF GERMAN HISTORY.

Library of Congress Catalog Card Number: 58-59832

Printed February 1965

Table of Contents

Introduction

"1848 was the turning point at which modern history failed to turn." So runs the famous dictum of G. M. Trevelyan, the renowned English historian, summing up the revolutionary movements of the mid-nineteenth century.

Such a statement immediately raises fundamental problems about the very nature of history: Does history move inevitably in certain directions? Can history be personified and said to be consciously following a certain route, as the great German philosopher Hegel would have it? Can history be regarded in such humanized terms that it might be considered capable of misreading the signposts and thus fail to take the proper turns? And if this be so, can the historian claim to *know* in which direction history may be moving? Can he determine when history is following along its preordained track or is temporarily derailed?

Fascinating as such abstract speculations regarding the nature of history and historical knowledge may be, it would probably be wrong to read such implications into Trevelyan's well-known remark. Instead, he was merely summarizing in metaphorical terms his interpretation of the events of 1848 in relation to preceding and subsequent events. Believing that political and social developments during the first half of the nineteenth century had made it possible for mankind to turn from despotism to freedom, Trevelyan found the insurrectionary outbursts of 1848 to represent a crucial point in such a transition; to him the reestablishment of autocratic rule throughout Europe in the 1850's indicated that although 1848 seemed destined to be a turning point — in fact, history failed to turn.

But not all historians would agree with Trevelyan's interpretation of the developments leading up to the revolutions of 1848 and their impact on the subsequent course of events. Indeed, it is precisely on these points that historians differ most in their views of the meaning and significance of 1848, and it is on this very question of historical interpretation that this selection of readings is focused. Making use of Trevelyan's metaphorical concepts we are here concerned chiefly with the following questions: If history can be said to travel along certain lines, just exactly what path was it following prior to 1848? Was 1848 a possible turning-point or a mere halt by the side of the road? If history did change its course in 1848, did it turn in the direction anticipated by the historians? The answers to these questions are not simple, for they require knowledge and understanding not only of the events of the 1848 period themselves, but also of their connection with the developments before and after this brief era of revolutionary outbreaks.

If, on January 1, 1848, a man in the street had been asked, "Which way is Europe going?" he might well have replied, "Nowhere in particular," for the social and political map of Europe appeared much the same as it had been after the Congress of Vienna in 1815. With the exception of France, Belgium, and England (where political changes in the 1830's had resulted in the establishment of liberal but not democratic states), most of Europe lived under regimes of political repression, autocratic government, and aristocratic privilege; and the more one advanced towards the east and south of Europe, the more the Old Regime of the Eighteenth Century revealed itself intact.

The independent German states were often referred to as "the Germanies," since there was no unified Germany; the German Confederation (*Deutscher Bund*) existed only in the form of a conference of ambassadors dominated by Metternich and a political police force also under his control. Italy was no more than "a geographical expression," for it also consisted of a number of independent states with Metternich as the "coachman," directing the destinies of the Italian peninsula as he did those of the Germanies. Furthermore, the great autocratic states of Russia, Austria, and Prussia conserved the Old Regime in all its political and social manifestations.

A more astute observer, however, might have perceived serious weaknesses in the apparently intact Restoration system created at the Vienna Congress. For one thing, the great powers no longer acted in unison. The Concert of Europe, created by the Tsar, Metternich, and Castlereagh in order to maintain the 1815 settlement, was shaken when England refused to cooperate in putting down liberal uprisings in the 1820's and 1830's and had been further weakened when France overthrew the restored Bourbon regime and established a liberal monarchy in 1830. More threatening to the stability of Metternich's Europe, however, were the pressures arising from liberalism, nationalism, and the economic changes brought about by the growing Industrial Revolution.

Liberalism — with its emphasis on the replacement of autocratic governments by constitutional states under the rule of law — had become the creed of the bourgeoisie who regarded its principles as a theoretical justification for their claims to political power. Nationalism, stimulated by the Romantic movement which had aroused the interest of various ethnic groups in their common past, had also grown. Those peoples suppressed by foreign rule or living under separate governments wished to be united in their own national state. Nationalism was closely allied with liberalism, for the middle class used both these doctrines as weapons to overthrow autocratic regimes and to achieve its own objectives. It was automatically assumed that once subject or disunited nationalities achieved independent states of their own, they would adopt liberal constitutions.

These liberal and national movements varied in strength and emphasis throughout Europe, depending largely on the power of the bourgeoisie and the political and social diversities of the respective states. In France, for example, national unity had been achieved centuries earlier, so the revolutionary tide in 1848 concentrated largely on liberal political changes and the social problems of the working class. In Germany and Italy, however, the pressure for change was both national and liberal, for these countries hoped to achieve their national unification within the framework of liberal governments. In the Hapsburg territories of eastern Europe, on the other hand, the movement was national rather than liberal, owing to the weakness of the bourgeoisie in that area and to the fact that the freedom from Hapsburg domination took precedence over constitutional questions among the subject nationalities.

Economic changes reinforced the liberal and national movement, for the nascent Industrial Revolution had strengthened the bourgeoisie, its chief supporters. At the same time, the urban proletariat, suffering from the horrors of the early factory system, sought to ameliorate their condition by social reforms which, they thought, could be achieved by liberal and democratic political changes. It is not surprising, then, that the 1848 insurrections focused on political, national, and social questions.

Already in 1820 and, more explosively, in 1830, there had been liberal and national outbreaks against the autocratic regimes imposed by the Congress of Vienna. Although Metternich and his allies had been able in most cases to put down the insurrections and restore reactionary rule, the pressures which had given rise to these disturbances continued to exist and to grow from 1830 to 1848.

These forces working against Metternich's Europe were augmented by an economic depression beginning in 1846 and deepening during the succeeding two years. A threefold crisis — agricultural, industrial, and financial — added misery to existing political grievances and increased the demand for changes. Metternich himself was aware that the current of history was moving away from his aim to maintain stable and reactionary governments, for in October, 1847, he remarked: "I am an old doctor; I can distinguish a passing illness from a mortal ailment. We are in the throes of the latter." To Metternich, liberalism and nationalism were diseases attacking the body politic, and he had good reason to fear that the reactionary Europe he had helped to create after 1815 was about to succumb to the revolutionary virus.

Within six months, Metternich's diagnosis seemed borne out. Insurrections swept through Europe, princes trembled and had to make liberal concessions; Metternich himself was forced to flee. While Metternich considered the revolutionary forces fatal to Europe, the revolutionaries saw 1848 as the "springtime of nations." To them, history was moving toward a new era of freedom, liberty, and happiness for all mankind.

Events in Paris, the traditional center of European political agitation, had stimulated outbreaks throughout Europe. There, at the end of February, 1848, an uprising ousted the Liberal Monarchy of Louis-Philippe and instituted the Second French Republic with universal manhood suffrage and a government guarantee of "the right to work" for the laboring man. The insurrection in Paris set off a revolutionary "chain reaction." Within a few weeks revolutions had broken out in Vienna, Berlin, Milan, Budapest — indeed, in all the German and Italian states and throughout the Hapsburg domains.

In general, the events throughout Europe during 1848 followed the same pattern and, with minor variations, went through identical phases:

(1) In the spring of 1848, the revolutionary cause seemed successful everywhere. As we have seen, a republic replaced the monarchy in France. The rulers of the German and Italian states as well as the powerful Hapsburg emperor were forced to grant liberal constitutions to their subjects. Even more striking was the fact that the Italians seemed well on their way to achieving national unity, while the German states sent representatives to a National Assembly at Frankfurt where the constitution for a unified Germany was to be worked out. Furthermore, the Magyars and Czechs within the Hapsburg Empire were given liberal grants of autonomy and national freedom. This unrivalled series of revolutionary triumphs seemed to have wiped clean the slate of the past and set about the writing of a new chapter in European history.

(2) During the summer of 1848, the weaknesses of the insurrectionary forces became evident as the revolutionary movements underwent a series of internal crises. It is always easier to overthrow the past than to construct the future, and the divisions which appeared among the leaders of the liberal and national causes in the various countries soon made this fact clear. In France, bloody street-fighting in the "June Days" between the working-class element and the moderate bourgeoisie broke up the victorious coalition which had thrown out Louis-Philippe and established the Republic. In Italy, jealousy among the rulers of the smaller states weakened their military operations against Austria, and in Germany the delegates to the Frankfurt Parliament lost precious time and alienated their supporters in arguing about the boundaries and

form of the unified German state they hoped to create.

(3) While the revolutionaries disputed among themselves, the reactionaries gradually recovered their strength. By the end of 1848 the insurrectionary cause was endangered everywhere, and the years from 1849 to 1851 saw a complete reversal of the earlier revolutionary triumph. In France the fear of social upheaval and the "red spectre" led to the election of Prince Louis Napoleon, pretender to the Bonapartist throne, as President of the Republic, for it was believed he would uphold order and security. The Hapsburgs rescinded the liberal reforms they had granted in Vienna and Prague and, with the assistance of the Russians and the Croats, overthrew the Magyar republic which Louis Kossuth had created in Hungary. As a last desperate measure, Italian radicals deposed their princes and proclaimed short-lived republics, all too soon overthrown by foreign troops, mainly Austrian. And in Germany, the Frankfurt Parliament finally presented a constitution in March, 1849, offering the imperial crown of a united Germany, which did not include Austria, to the king of Prussia. This offer was refused by the Hohenzollern monarch who neither wished to antagonize Austria nor to become ruler of a parliamentary state. Within a short time Prussian troops together with Austrian forces, now freed from the task of re-subjugating the rebellious Hapsburg realms and Italy, invaded those German states where radical regimes had been installed, restoring the German princelings to full autocratic powers as during the Metternich era.

If, then, in 1851 our mythical man in the street had been asked in which direction European history had travelled during the three preceding years, he might well have denied that there had been any progress at all, except possibly backwards. In eastern and central Europe, reaction reigned supreme, for the Hapsburgs had re-established autocratic rule in their own domains as well as regaining their hegemony in Germany

and Italy. All was back to where it had been before 1848; Metternichism had returned, though without Metternich. Nationalist movements fared no better than had the liberal cause. Dreams of a united Italy had to be postponed until the Italians could acquire a powerful ally to match the military strength of Austria. Similarly, the hopes for a united Germany under liberal auspices had failed, and the way was paved for the unification of Germany under Bismarck's policy of "blood and iron" during the 1860's. Even in France, the starting point of the revolutionary spree, fears of social upheaval had made the people willingly exchange liberty for order and entrust the executive power to a man whose name symbolized dictatorship and who, in a few years time, was to restore the Napoleonic Empire. Liberalism, nationalism, the desire for social reform — all the currents leading to the insurrectionary tidal wave of 1848 — had apparently failed to change the course of European history.

But had they failed completely or forever? The next two decades were to see the national unifications of both Italy and Germany, and the twentieth century saw the breakup of the multi-national Hapsburg Empire into its national components, as foreshadowed in 1848. While Napoleon III's imperial dictatorship reversed the progress of liberalism, France eventually returned to its course of democratic evolution, and republican political institutions were gradually to predominate throughout Europe during the twentieth century. Similarly, the social question, summarily disposed of during 1848, was to be pressed with increasing urgency until the masses were given a share in political power and the state became an instrument for bettering the conditions of the workers. Thus many of the demands of the insurrectionists of 1848 were ultimately to be attained, although in some cases these achieved a warped and twisted fulfillment far removed from the ideas entertained by their proponents in 1848.

By now it should be clear that the interpretation of 1848 as a "turning point" will depend not only on how one regards the revolutionary movements themselves, but also on one's views as to how, or in what direction, history was moving both before and after 1848. If 1848 is viewed as a point where Europe could have turned in the direction of greater liberty and freedom for the masses but instead relapsed into conservative and reactionary rule, then it was a turning point where history did indeed fail to turn, in accordance with Trevelyan's dictum. If, however, one believes the liberal and national goals of the 1848 movements were achieved later in the nineteenth and twentieth century, then 1848 represents a premature attempt and only a temporary setback in the path of historical evolution. Or one can differentiate among the aims of 1848: while liberalism suffered a defeat, certain aspects of nationalism were actually encouraged when conservative elements took advantage of the force inherent in the national ideal to consolidate or extend their power.

There are many other possible interpretations. Those historians who consider the nineteenth century primarily as a time when the power of the national state increased, not necessarily along liberal lines, might tend to see 1848 as a point where this growth was accelerated rather than halted. Or, if the 1848 revolutions are regarded solely as a movement of the middle class to attain power, then they might be considered a failure. On the other hand, if certain events are looked upon as constituting an awakening of the proletariat, then 1848 becomes a turning point of no small significance. For it is here that the "social question," as propounded by Marx and Engels, first gropes toward articulate expression.

The task of interpreting 1848 is complicated still further by the fact that the outbreaks, despite their contemporaneity, varied so much from one country to the next, passing through so many different phases within each country, that the analysis given by any one historian must of necessity depend on his personal vision of nineteenth-

century history and influence his choice of emphasis. The excerpts in this volume illustrate how the disagreements of leading historians about 1848 arise in large measure as a result of divergent historical perspectives.

In the case of France, for example, developments of the nineteenth century are usually related to that climactic event of French history — the French Revolution. Was the Revolution of 1848 in France a continuation, a fulfillment, an extension, or a reversal of 1789? To Sir Lewis B. Namier, the English historian, "The principles of equality and national sovereignty, bequeathed by the Great Revolution, found in 1848 their logical fulfilment in universal suffrage and the Republic." Lord Elton, on the other hand, considers 1848 as a new, economic revolution aiming at a redistribution of wealth. Whereas the "old" French Revolution had been a national movement, this "new" revolution was the work of one class, the urban proletariat. But this fact has been obscured, he claims, because the residue of the old Revolution, the demand for its logical completion by the establishment of a Republic, survived and became intermixed with the distinctive elements of the new of 1848. In the end, Elton states, the French people chose Louis-Napoleon who stood for the preservation of the old Revolution and the destruction of the new — but the forces of the old Revolution were spent, and the new Revolution was to make itself felt later in French history.

While J. P. T. Bury recognizes "the conflict between those who want to seize the opportunity to solve the social problem by radical reforms of the conditions of labour and those who are determined to resist social changes which they fear will lead to chaos and anarchy," he points out that "the number of Frenchmen who genuinely desired a social revolution and the abolition of economic inequality was comparatively small." After the June Days the insurrection of 1848 retreated from its social aspirations and "harked back to the traditions of the Great Revolution." The chief difference between 1789 and 1848, according to Bury, lies in the fact that the great mass of the nation which had provided the revolutionary force in 1789 had become satisfied by the abolition of feudal privileges and political inequality; by 1848 they were a conservative, possessing class rather than the disinherited.

Although interpretation of 1848 in France focuses in its relationship to the Great French Revolution of 1789, the role of 1848 in German history involves a judgment on the strength, effectiveness, and character of the forces of liberalism and nationalism among the German people. Looking back from the mid-twentieth century in the light of recent German aggressiveness, two English historians, A. J. P. Taylor and Lewis B. Namier, tend to deny the strength of liberal sentiments among the Germans and to emphasize the idea of nationalistic power as the core of German feeling. Indeed, Namier derides 1848 as "the revolution of the intellectuals," who proved more nationalistic than liberal in sentiment, for they denied to Czechs, Poles, and Danes the right they demanded for themselves. Taylor claims that the German people missed their chance to follow along a liberal path and returned to the idea of force as their dominant motif after 1848. William Ebenstein, a political scientist of Princeton University, also emphasizes the weakness of the German liberals and ascribes their failure to the two-front war which the middle classes waged "against the feudal Junkers and absolute kings above and against the working class below."

Opposed to the views expressed by Namier and Taylor are two outstanding German historians, Veit Valentin and Frederick Meinecke. Although admitting the failure of the liberal movement in 1848, these men do not impugn the motives of the German liberals nor castigate them for being more nationalistic than liberal, as did Taylor and Namier. Instead, Valentin stresses the strength of liberal sentiment in Germany in 1848 and points out the real contributions made by the liberals despite their defeat. To Valentin, the chief fault of the revolutionaries lay in their use of inappropriate methods to achieve their ends. But the spirit of the revolution remained, despite its external failure—it was the method of working which was defeated, not the liberal idea. Meinecke endeavors to show that the defeat of German liberalism was inevitable, due to a variety of circumstances arising from the peculiar nature of past German political developments, and that the fault is not to be laid at the door of liberal sentiment, which still persisted in Germany.

Hans Rothfels, a leading German historian who taught for a time at the University of Chicago, also disagrees with Taylor and Namier. Their interpretations are faulty, he claims, due to their misconception of the nature of liberal and nationalistic doctrines in the mid-nineteenth century as well as to their failure to appreciate the difficulties inherent in the predicament of the liberals in the Frankfurt Parliament. Despite the superficial defeat suffered by the German liberals, 1848 was a genuine turning point involving basic political and social forces.

The great English historian, G. P. Gooch, may be said to view events in 1848 as putting a halt to certain developments while accelerating others: German liberalism, he claims, was given a death blow, but the revolutions were "a milestone" along Germany's path to national unification, a continuing process during the nineteenth century.

When an attempt is made to estimate the general results of 1848 throughout Europe, interpretations again differ. While, to Namier, "the Revolution of the Intellectuals" left its imprint only in the realm of ideas, others claim it had profound practical consequences. François Fejtö, for example, finds 1848 a turning point, "both a beginning and an end." While the revolutionaries might have failed temporarily and superficially in the pursuit of their ideas and aims, the predominant themes of the revolution (which he defines as socialism, democracy, nationalism, and internationalism) were given new life and importance in European history thenceforth. For one thing, the dichotomy between middle-class aspirations and the desire of the workers for social reform first became clear.

Priscilla Robertson, on the other hand, minimizes the effect of the 1848 outbreaks. Her criterion for the effectiveness of any revolution rests on its ability to "shake up society" into a new pattern gaining new freedoms. This, she says, did not happen in 1848. Rothfels, however, claims that the European pattern was changed so fundamentally that society could not and did not return to pre-1848 conditions.

Bernadotte E. Schmitt, Professor Emeritus of History at the University of Chicago and an expert on European diplomatic history, finds 1848 not so much a turning point as a terminus. Although an instance of arrested historical development, 1848 had profound consequences for history precisely because of its failure. Writing a century after the revolutions, Schmitt endeavors to show how the failures of 1848 affected the future of Europe up to and including the present. Indeed, Schmitt finds many parallels between the problems facing Europe then and now.

This study of the meaning and significance of the 1848 revolutions, then, is not of antiquarian interest only. Rather, it provides a key for the comprehension of European developments from 1848 to the present, and for a better understanding of our contemporary world. To the student of history, furthermore, it should give insight into the complicated nature of historical change and the problems of historical interpretation.

[NOTE: In the selections that follow the editor has thought it advisable to leave all spelling, grammar, and punctuation as they appeared in the original publications from which they were taken.]

First Stage: The Revolution Triumphs; February–May, 1848.

1848	FEBRUARY 22–24	Demonstrations in Paris, leading to abdication of Louis-Philippe; installation of Provisional Government and proclamation of Second French Republic.
	FEBRUARY 27	Demonstrations and rioting break out in German and Italian cities.
	MARCH 4	Piedmont accorded a constitution (the "Statuto") by its ruler.
	MARCH 11–15	Disturbances in Prague, Vienna, Budapest; Metternich forced to flee; Hapsburg Emperor promises constitution; Hungary given virtual independence.
	MARCH 15–21	Intermittent demonstrations and street fighting in Berlin lead king of Prussia to promise constitution and to support moves for German national unity. Riots and insurrections force rulers of other German states to do the same.
	MARCH 18–22	Disturbances in Milan, leading to ousting of Austrian forces.
	MARCH 22	Proclamation of Venetian Republic. Piedmont declares war on Austria.
	APRIL	Hapsburg Emperor promises constitution for Bohemia. Uprisings in Moravia, Galicia, Dalmatia, and Transylvania. Insurrections in Poland for independence.
	APRIL 29	Pope announces neutrality in national war against Austria; papal troops withdrawn from Italian forces.
	MAY 15	Collapse of revolution in Naples; withdrawal of Neapoliton troops from Italian forces.
	MAY 18	Meeting of Frankfurt Parliament (Nationalversammlung) to achieve German unity.

Second Stage: The Revolutions Run into Difficulties; June–December, 1848.

	JUNE 2	Opening of first Pan-Slav Congress in Prague.
	JUNE 12–17	Windischgrätz bombards Prague, crushes Czech revolution, and establishes martial law in Bohemia, marking first step in Hapsburg recovery of power.
	JUNE 23–26	Bloody street fighting in Paris after the dissolution of the National Workshops. Severe reaction follows.
	JULY 24	Battle of Custozza: Piedmontese and other Italian forces defeated by Austrians, and Hapsburg power reestablished in Lombardy.
	SEPTEMBER 17	Jellachich, governor of Croatia, invades Hungary under grant of authority from Hapsburg ruler. Hungarians drive him out and invade Austria.
	OCTOBER 31	Windischgrätz re-takes Vienna from radicals.
	NOVEMBER 16–25	Popular insurrection in Rome forces Pope Pius IX to flee city.

DECEMBER 2	Abdication of Emperor Ferdinand of Austria and accession of Francis Joseph I (1848–1916).
DECEMBER 10	Prince Louis Napoleon Bonaparte elected president of the French Republic.

Third Stage: The Reactionaries Triumph; 1849–1851.

1849	FEBRUARY 9	Proclamation of Roman Republic.
	MARCH 4–7	Austrian Reichstag dissolved, and Emperor promulgates constitution retaining his autocratic powers and depriving Hungary of autonomy.
	MARCH 23	Piedmontese defeated by Austrians at battle of Novara after renewing war against Austria. King Charles Albert abdicates as king of Piedmont-Sardinia in favor of son, Victor Emmanuel II.
	MARCH 27	Frankfurt Parliament issues constitution creating a federal state with responsible parliamentary government and offers crown to King Frederick William of Prussia.
	APRIL 13–14	Hungarians proclaim independence and form Hungarian Republic with Kossuth as president.
	APRIL 28	King Frederick William IV refuses crown offered him by Frankfurt Assembly, which collapses.
	JUNE	Emperor Francis Joseph accepts the offer of Tsar Nicholas of Russia to aid in suppression of the Hungarian revolution.
	JULY 1	Fall of Roman Republic to French troops. French Assembly, under conservative domination, had authorized French intervention against the Roman Republic.
	JULY 20– AUGUST 28	Siege and bombardment of Venice, which succumbs to Austrian troops who had earlier reestablished the Tuscan ruler.
	AUGUST	Hungarian revolution defeated by combined Austro-Russian military efforts.
		Revolutionary movement quelled throughout Italian peninsula, Hapsburg domains, and German states.
1850	JANUARY 21	Prussian king grants constitution with pseudo-liberal features.
	MARCH 20	Prussia attempts to establish German Union by meeting at Erfurt of representatives of princes.
	NOVEMBER 29	The Capitulation of Olmütz. Prussia gives in to Austrian pressure and abandons attempt to unite Germany. The German Confederation is reestablished in its original form.
1851	DECEMBER 2	Coup d'état by Louis Napoleon in France, establishing his dictatorship. The following year the Second Republic gives way to the Second Empire.
	DECEMBER 31	Austria's constitution suppressed; return to complete absolutism.

The Conflict of Opinion

"1848 was the turning point at which modern history failed to turn."

— G. M. Trevelyan

"Failure or not, 1848 was a genuine turning point. The year 1850 no more restored 1847 than 1815 had returned to 1788. . . . What had been, in the main, an autocratic society, domestically or internationally, was consolidated or fell apart into more strongly centralized or nationalized fragments — a process which was concomitant with the growing influence of the middle class."

— Hans Rothfels

"Some revolutions shake up society so that when the pieces fall together again they are in a new pattern which permits growth in a new direction. In 1848 that hardly happened. . . . The test of whether a revolution is successful is not whether some power with a new name exercises the same essential restraints as before . . . but whether some important group has won some important new freedom — economic, political, social, or religious. Out of 1848 and its struggles no important new freedom was wrested."

— Priscilla Robertson

"Eighteen forty-eight in the history of Europe and the world, marks the spread of new ideas and new aims, which thenceforth become common property. If we look at the revolution from the point of view of its ideas and aims, we can say that the reactionaries only appeared to be the victors in 1848 and 1849. . . . Socialism, democracy, nationalism in its best sense, and internationalism in the sense of a recognition of the nation's interdependence: those were the predominant themes of the revolutions of 1848. Like all revolutions, they marked both a beginning and an end."

— François Fejtö

"Throughout 1848 the ultimate control of the state-machine, and still more of the armies of the Great Powers on the European Continent, remained with the Conservatives. . . . The 'Revolution of the Intellectuals' exhausted itself without achieving concrete results: it left its imprint only in the realm of ideas."

— Louis B. Namier

"Unsuccessful though the risings had been, their very failure had profound consequences for Europe, some of which may still be felt in the present troubled world."

— Bernadotte E. Schmitt

1848—AS SEEN FROM 1948

BERNADOTTE E. SCHMITT

The year 1948 marked the centennial of the revolutions of 1848 and prompted many historians to review the events of that year in terms of the added historical perspective given by the passage of time. Dr. Bernadotte E. Schmitt, Professor Emeritus of Modern History at the University of Chicago and editor of the *Journal of Modern History* for seventeen years, sought to trace the influence of the developments of 1848 on the contemporary world. He is particularly concerned with the impact of internal developments in the European countries on international relations, for he has long been an expert on European diplomatic affairs. Not only has he written important works on the origins of the First World War, but he has also served as Editor-in-Chief of the *Documents on German Foreign Policy, 1918–1945* and is currently a historical adviser to the State Department. In the following selection, a paper read to the American Philosophical Society in November, 1948, Schmitt indicates that many of the problems present in 1848 remain unsolved today.

A HUNDRED years have passed since the great upheaval commonly called the Revolution of 1848. If the old distinction is still valid between revolt and revolution, that is, between unsuccessful and successful risings against constituted authority, then what happened in 1848 had better be termed a revolt. For, although during the first few months the risings were generally successful against established governments, reaction soon set in, the revolutionary forces were gradually overcome or simply petered out, and by the end of 1849, the old order had been in large measure restored, at least outwardly. But unsuccessful though the risings had been, their very failure had profound consequences for Europe, some of which may still be felt in the present troubled world.

The three years which have passed since the close of hostilities in 1945 have witnessed immense difficulties, political, economic, and social, in France, Italy, Germany, and central and southeastern Europe. Except for Greece, Bulgaria, and Serbia, it was this same area in which the tumults and shoutings of 1848 took place; and just as in 1948 England had remained calm and stable and Soviet Russia is a land of silent mystery, so in 1848 there was in England, instead of revolution, only an innocuous business called the Chartist Movement which hardly disturbed even the surface of English life (so that Louis Philippe and Guizot, the Prince of Prussia and Metternich fled to London as matter of course), and tsarist Russia boasted of the "tranquillity," which, as enforced by the famous "third section" of the police (a pale anticipation of the NKVD), distinguished that land from the "chaos" of the West.

In early 1848 revolution was "in the air." Political discontent, ranging from demands for a wider suffrage which would under-

From *Proceedings of the American Philosophical Society*, Vol. 93, No. 3, June, 1949, pp. 216–221. By permission of the author and of the American Philosophical Society.

mine middle-class rule (France) to hatred of the autocratic systems restored after 1815 (Central Europe), had been simmering for a considerable time, and the revolutionary movement which broke out in Sicily early in January served as a spark to the chain of power which exploded in one capital after another. The spread of the new processes of manufacturing and transportation — the so-called industrial revolution — from England to the Continent, which had reached considerable dimensions in France and penetrated even to Austria and Italy, had led to much distress among the poorer classes of society, that is, to long hours of work, low wages, atrocious factories, dreary houses, and numerous other evils. In various parts of Europe, the crops had been poor in 1847, so that by midwinter there was considerable distress in many cities. Nor had there been lacking during the previous decade political agitators and social reformers who kept prodding both the prosperous middle classes and the miserable working classes to action.

Yet the actual outbreaks often came from insignificant causes. In Paris it was the decision of the government to prohibit a political banquet that sent the mob into the streets and precipitated the fall of the Orleans monarchy and the establishment of a provisional government; it was a speech in Budapest that led Vienna to rise against Metternich and paralyze the Austrian government; in Germany it was a handful of private persons who organized the *Vorparlament* that challenged the Confederation of 1815. It would be hard to say who was the more surprised by the events of February–March 1848 — the governments that were so easily toppled over or the inexperienced politicians and enthusiastic crowds that gave them the push.

Be that as it may, by midsummer 1848 a Second Republic had been proclaimed in France and an Assembly elected by universal manhood suffrage was drafting a new constitution. Constituent bodies were sitting in Frankfort, Berlin, and Vienna and liberal ministries were at the helm. Ancient diets had taken on new life in Budapest and Zagreb. In Italy four states had been granted constitutions by their terrified rulers. Even in the distant Danubian Principalities (as Romania was then called) the powers of the hospodars had been somewhat modified.

Europe, then, seemed on the verge of a new dispensation. The expectation was widespread that there would emerge constitutional governments based on universal manhood suffrage, through the functioning of which all classes of society would be able to present their demands and secure redress of grievances. There was also confidence, or at least hope, that the apparent acceptance of the principle of nationality would result in the establishment of a strong Germany replacing the weak Confederation, to the creation of a united Italy, and to recognition of the national identities of the Magyars and the various Slavic peoples of Austria. For a brief moment some persons even dreamed of a restoration of Poland. Alas! These hopes were to be dashed as miserably as were our own dreams in 1919 and again in 1945 of a just and lasting peace.

In France the Second Republic was undone by two circumstances. In the first place, under working-class pressure, the Provisional Government, manned by liberal Republicans, had established the National Workshops, which were viewed by their supporters as the first step toward socialism. The workshops were badly managed — according to some, deliberately so, in order to discredit such a socialistic experiment — and became so futile and so expensive that the government determined to suppress them. But the proletariat resisted and much blood was shed before the government triumphed. These "June days" terrified both the middle classes and the peasants and turned them against liberalism and the "Jacobin" republic.

Secondly, this bitter struggle seemed to prove the necessity of a strong executive, and consequently the constitution adopted by the Assembly provided for a President with large powers who was to be elected by the people. The Assembly failed, however, to declare members of families that had reigned in France to be ineligible for the Presidency, and so great was the fear of socialism and so clever had been the misrepresentation of the Napoleonic Empire by its legatee, Prince Louis Napoleon, that it proved easy for that enigmatic person, who in April had served as a constable in Trafalgar Square in London during the Chartist demonstrations, to get himself elected President of the French Republic in December. In the government which he then set up, not one of the men who had formed the Provisional Government of February found a place.

In December 1851, the Prince-President overthrew the constitution and established a regime which we would now call authoritarian and which gave him vast personal powers. A year later the Second Republic was formally replaced by the Second Empire. Only manhood suffrage survived as a relic of the revolution of February 1848, and it was rendered innocuous by constitutional tricks copied from the First Empire.

These events of 1848–1852 explain much in the France of 1948. While the June days scotched socialism for the moment, the Communist Manifesto, written by Karl Marx and Friedrich Engels in February 1848, although it had no effect on the outbreak or the course of the revolution, was duly translated into French, and it gradually replaced, for the French working classes, the earlier socialist propaganda of Louis Blanc and Co. The first International, founded by Marx, was warmly supported in France; Marx, in turn, praised the Paris Commune 1871. In 1948 the Communist Manifesto provides the fundamental doctrine of the Communist party, which is the largest political group in France.

Furthermore, Louis Napoleon's *coup d'état* in 1851 is largely responsible for the French reluctance to see a strong executive power established. The constitutions of the Third Republic of 1875 and of the Fourth

Republic of 1946 testify to the fear of a man on horseback. Undoubtedly a great obstacle to General de Gaulle's becoming the ruler of France is the instinctive feeling of large numbers of Frenchmen that he seems too much like Louis Napoleon, who offered the country glory — and led it to disaster.

Thus the two problems which confronted France in 1848 — how to establish a stable balance between legislature and executive, and how to deal with serious social unrest — remain unsolved in 1948.

In Central Europe in 1848 the aims of the several revolutions were confused and sometimes conflicting. In Germany, which was then organized in a loose Confederation of thirty-nine states comparable to the United States under the Articles of Confederation, there was one people, the German, who, so far as it was politically conscious, aspired to a strong national state with a constitutional and monarchical government comparable to that which had just been overthrown in France. The Frankfort Parliament was the symbol of this German dream. In the Austrian Empire, on the other hand, eleven peoples lived under one government and, generally speaking, aspired to autonomy.

The two problems were not independent but closely related.

(a) Since there were many Germans in the Austrian Empire (chiefly in the provinces of Upper and Lower Austria), the establishment of a German national state which contained all the Germans would involve the disruption of the Austrian Empire — which was of course anathema to the ruling House of Habsburg.

(b) *Vice versa*, if the Austrian Empire were maintained intact, German unity could not be realized.

(c) If the Austrian Empire were included in the new Germany, then Germany would contain a large number of non-Germans.

If (a) were adopted, the so-called *grossdeutsch* solution, then the wedge of Bohemia lying between Silesia and Austria in which the Slavic Czechs predominated, would offer an additional problem. Since, however, neither the Czechs nor the Habsburg dynasty would hear of the inclusion of Bohemia in Germany, it was not in 1848 a practical proposition.

(c) would have been acceptable to the Habsburgs, but to no one else, and was not seriously considered.

Consequently, the Frankfort Parliament fell back on (b), the so-called *kleindeutsch* solution, and voted to establish a German Empire, minus any of the Habsburg lands, with the King of Prussia as Emperor. But this was rejected by both Prussia and Austria.

What then was left as possible? Obviously, the restoration of the *status quo ante,* that is, the maintenance of the Austrian Empire and the continuance of the German Confederation. Once the Austrian government had recovered from the paralysis and fright engendered by the upheaval of March 1848, it showed great resolution and cleverness in dealing with the inexperienced Frankfort Parliament, which contained an extraordinary number of pedagogues and pedants, and with the vacillating King of Prussia. In 1849 it brought about the end of the Frankfort Parliament before that body had established the new Germany, and in 1850 it imposed on Prussia the restoration of the Confederation.

So Germany obtained neither unity nor constitutional government. The only tangible result of the revolution was the constitution issued by the King of Prussia in 1850. This remarkable document left the executive power in the hands of the King; it established a parliament of two houses, the lower to be elected by manhood suffrage — but it reduced that suffrage to a joke by dividing the voters into three classes, according to the amount of taxes paid. Since the rich constituted the first class and the well-to-do the second class, they obtained control of the legislature at the expense of the third class, to which the rest of the people belonged who paid little in the way of taxes. By this antidemocratic

device, the Prussian government hoped to satisfy the propertied classes and the liberals, while at the same time denying any real power to the masses.

As a matter of fact, neither German unity nor political democracy made a deep appeal in 1848. The German peasantry and the several armies remained loyal to the reigning princes and exhibited little sympathy with what an English historian has aptly called the "revolution of the intellectuals." While the Communist Manifesto, which was written by two Germans and reached Germany by June 1848, appears to have had little or no effect on the unorganized working classes, nevertheless, workers' demonstrations in Berlin, an open revolt in Vienna against the Assembly, and an abortive attack on the Frankfort Parliament made clear that the German radicals were demanding something more than constitutional government and manhood suffrage. All of these demonstrations of the left were easily suppressed, but the middle-class liberals, who were the backbone of the Frankfort Parliament, became alarmed, and from this time on — the autumn of 1848 — the reaction had easier going, as was evidenced by the appointment of conservative ministries in both Berlin and Vienna and the dissolution of the Prussian constituent Assembly.

Yet the very failure of this first German bid for *Einheit, Freiheit, Macht* paved the way for success twenty years later. One of the most acute observers of the upheaval of 1848 was a young Prussian squire named Otto von Bismarck, and when he became minister-president of Prussia in 1862, he did not hesitate to proclaim that German unity could not be achieved by parliamentary majorities, that is, by the technique of the Frankfort Parliament, but required methods of blood and iron. He was also clear in his own mind that the territorial question could be solved only by the exclusion of Austria, even though this meant excluding from Germany the German population of Austria. With almost diabolical cleverness he manipulated the Prussian constitution of 1850 to suit his purposes, even though he became thereby the most hated man in Germany. How he provoked and won the three wars with Denmark, Austria, and France need not be repeated here. Suffice it to say that the German Empire proclaimed in January 1871 was identical territorially with that proposed by the Frankfort Parliament.

On the other hand, the liberal state envisaged at Frankfort was discarded. After winning the wars against Denmark and Austria, Bismarck invited the Prussian Diet to pass an act of indemnity for his violations of the constitution, and the Diet complied: never again did the Diet seriously challenge the power of the Crown. Bismarck did feel the necessity of establishing a national parliament for the Empire, the Reichstag, elected by universal manhood suffrage, but he saw to it that the powers of the Reichstag were limited and that it served primarily as a debating society. Furthermore, whereas King Frederick William IV in 1848 had proclaimed that "Prussia is henceforth merged in Germany," Bismarck arranged that undemocratic and military Prussia became the predominant power in Germany. In short, Bismarck did his best to eliminate from the German Empire the liberal and democratic ideas of 1848; he did not succeed altogether, but the German course was certainly steered in the direction of authoritarianism, away from the generous concepts of Frankfort.

The Iron Chancellor so successfully manipulated both the Kaiser and the Reichstag that the defects in the constitution of 1871 were not apparent until after his removal from office, after which Germany and the world had to put up with the vagaries of the dilettante who was William II. The inadequacy of the system for dealing with the new forces of social democracy became more and more evident, and there is reason to believe that fear of socialism entered into the calculations of the German government when in 1914 it took the fatal plunge into war.

When Germany was defeated in 1918, the Bismarckian state and the Hohenzollern monarchy collapsed together. This German collapse and the simultaneous disintegration of the Austro-Hungarian state raised once more the questions of 1848: (1) how to establish a German democracy? and (2) what to do with German Austria?

The men who drafted the Weimar constitution of 1919 were the spiritual heirs of 1848, not only in their general approach to the problem but also in their determination to devise a perfect constitution. Unhappily, the Weimar Republic did not acquire a hold on the affections of the German people, partly no doubt because it had been imposed on them by the demand of President Wilson, but chiefly, in my opinion, because the Germans did not take kindly to the idea of governing themselves and found it convenient to blame the Treaty of Versailles rather than their own shortcomings. In any case, the Republic did not really resist being pushed over by the Nazis. Now that the Nazis have been beaten, we are back where we started in 1848 — only there is probably less genuine enthusiasm for democracy in Germany today than there was in 1848.

In 1919 German Austria was not allowed to join Germany, because this would profoundly alter the balance of power and the military situation in Europe. When Hitler annexed Austria in 1938, he effected the solution ruled out in 1848. But after their first enthusiasm had worn off, the Austrians themselves came to dislike the *Anschluss*. So the victorious Allies, in line with Austrian wishes and for the protection of their own interests, are committed in principle to the restoration of an independent Austria. But who knows whether Austria is capable of a truly independent existence?

Thus after a hundred years, the German problem, both political and territorial, is still with us. Moreover, Germany is now, what it was not in 1848, the most important economic factor in Western Europe, and obviously the political problems of Germany cannot be solved except in relation to the economic. If the period from

1815 to 1914 is now recognized to have been the British Century and if the American Century is supposed to date from 1917 or 1919, maybe we should speak of the would-be German Century from 1848 to 1945, during which the German question dominated the life in Europe.

Central Europe has proved as difficult a problem to solve as Germany. When the Metternich system broke down in 1848, Hungary was able to obtain a large measure of autonomy within the Habsburg state, under its ancient constitution somewhat revised. But the ruling group in Hungary, the Magyars, would not grant to the non-Magyar races, who outnumbered them, the same privileges which they had obtained from Austria, nor did they relieve the peasantry of the antiquated feudal dues surviving from the days of Joseph II. So presently the Magyars had to face rebellions against themselves — rebellions supported, it need hardly be remarked, by the government in Vienna. When in desperation they proclaimed the independence of Hungary, they only played into the hands of their enemies.

The Slavic groups under Habsburg rule, who were opposed as were the Magyars to the centralized control of Vienna, got so far as to organize a Slav Congress, the first of its kind, and to advocate a policy of federalism. It was at this time that the Czech leader and historian, Palacky, declared that, if Austria did not exist, it would have to be invented as a device for preserving the Slavs from German domination. In passing, it may be remarked that the Russian anarchist, Bakunin, in 1848 advocated a somewhat different solution of the Slavic problem — nothing less than the creation of a democratic federation extending from the Urals to the Adriatic (the satellite system of Soviet Russia in 1948 would make him shudder).

Neither the Magyar nor the Slavic program was sincerely accepted by the Vienna government, and after recovering first its nerves after the collapse of March and then its military strength after victories in Italy, it played off the rival races with great skill; and, although it had finally to call in Russian troops to defeat the Magyars, it was able, one by one, to suppress the several rebellions and in large measure to restore the old centralizing system. Perhaps the most striking fact was the ability of the government to defeat one racial group of the Empire with the soldiers of another. On this issue, the action of the government in abolishing the relics of feudalism in September 1848 was apparently decisive.

Curious enough, at one stage in its maneuvers, the government issued a constitution, the famous constitution of Kremsier, which recognized the principle of the equality of the nationalities and provided a sensible scheme of reorganizing the state. It is the considered judgment of many historians that had this remarkable instrument been allowed to go into effect, it might well have solved the problem of nationalities and made it possible for the Habsburg state to survive. In the hour of triumph, however, the government revoked it.

The defeat of the workers' rising in Vienna, already noted, and the abolition of feudal dues paralyzed the social forces which had erupted in March 1848. In Austria, no more than in France or Germany, was the Communist Manifesto an important factor in the march of events.

For ten years, from 1850 to 1860, the defeated nationalities and for that matter the Germans in Austria proper had to submit once more to Vienna, but in the latter year the restored regime, the "Bach system," broke down. Schemes of 1860 and 1861 were proposed and rejected. Finally, in 1867, a kind of compromise was reached for the benefit of Germans and Magyars at the expense of Slavs and Latins. For some years this Dualism, as it came to be called, was as superficially successful as the contemporary Bismarckian experiment in Germany. Yet by 1914 the Habsburg state was in such a parlous condition that foreign war seemed, to its ruling clique, the only escape from domestic discords. In the decision for war against Serbia, which was recognized to involve the danger of war with Russia, the hatred of Russia felt by the Magyars, who had not forgotten the Russian invasion of 1849, was an important factor.

In 1918 the Habsburg empire collapsed and dissolved into its component parts, six Succession States replacing the Dual Monarchy. At the time this solution appeared logical, and high hopes were entertained that at long last peace and prosperity would reign in Central Europe. Yet the actual results were very different. In the first place, hardly any of the new states was able to establish a sound economy, which became more and more evident during the Great Depression that began in 1929. Secondly, four of the six states contained intractable minorities, whose relations with the ruling races were never satisfactorily adjusted. So repeatedly during the twenty years between the two wars, critics of the settlements of 1919 repeated the aphorism of Palacky (without realizing that he had uttered it in quite different circumstances) that Austria must be invented, that is, restored.

From 1945 to 1948 the victorious Allies have been unable to agree on a solution of the problem of Central Europe. They are as divided as were the men of 1848. A *de facto* solution has been provided, temporarily, by the extension of Soviet power over nearly all of the area. Historically, of course, this Soviet expansion has little to justify it, and just as in the nineteenth century Russian Poland was never reconciled to tsarist rule and the Romanians always resented the periodic occupation of their lands by Russian armies, so now there are many signs that in all the Soviet satellites the Communist regimes depend upon force and have little popular support. In the course of a hundred years monarchial conservatism, democratic self-determination, and soviet communism have been successively tried in this vast area where both the war of 1914 and that of 1939 began, and the permanent solution has not yet been found.

Italy in 1848 was a geographical expression, without even the semblance of unity represented by the German Confederation. The governments were generally autocratic, and much of the peninsula was under Austrian influence or even direct Austrian rule. The Italians therefore faced the triple task of obtaining democratic government, creating some kind of national state, and driving out the hated foreigner — a truly formidable program. They made headway towards self-government through the constitutions granted in some of the states, and they organized a national war against Austria. But, weak, inexperienced, and not really united, they were twice defeated by the Austrian armies, and the last desperate efforts of the Venetian Republic and the Roman Republic, while full of glory, availed nothing. The only gain for the national cause was the proclamation of the Sardinian constitution of 1849 and the emergence of the House of Savoy as the hope of the future.

A decade later, the great Cavour almost miraculously achieved Italian unity on the basis of the Sardinian constitution. Down to 1914 Italy appeared to be making satisfactory progress towards democracy and to possess perhaps a more stable regime than France. Thanks to participating in the First World War, it obtained the irredentist territories that had been left to Austria in 1866. So in 1919 Italy had finally achieved the program of 1848.

The aspirations of Italy for expansion overseas, which helped to put Mussolini in power and ultimately led to defeat and disaster, have little relation to the ideas of 1848. It should be remembered, however, that hatred of Germany and Germans (represented in the nineteenth century by Austria) was centuries-old in Italy, and when in the game of empire *il duce* allied himself with *der Führer*, he was going against the deep-rooted instincts of his countrymen, so that it was psychologically easy for the Italians in 1943 to abandon the Axis and join the Allies.

The new Italian Republic is in tradition

with Mazzini and Garibaldi, both of whom played active roles in 1848. At this moment, November 1948, Italy has perhaps come nearer establishing a firm national state on a democratic basis than any of the other countries involved in the revolutions of 1848.

At several points in this paper, it has been remarked that in spite of the initial push given to the upheavals of 1848 by economic distress and social discontent, socialism made little appeal outside of certain urban centers and attempts to realize socialistic programs not only failed but played into the hands of reaction. In other words, the Communist Manifesto fell pretty flat. In passing, it may be noted that the events of 1848 did not seriously affect the economic life of Europe, for the peasants continued to grow their crops and industry, such as it was, did not cease to function. The immediate incentive to scrap private enterprise and substitute government production and distribution of the necessities of life was therefore lacking.

In 1948, however, Europe has only just begun to recover from the incredible devastation and economic chaos resulting from the most terrible war of modern times. It is not to be wondered at that the Communist Manifesto, especially as distorted by the Soviet Government and the Third Internationale, has attracted numerous followers in the heart of Europe.

In the hundred years under review Western liberalism has not been able to achieve political stability and economic security in Europe. German militarism was even less successful. Now Russian communism asks for its chance. We hope that it will not succeed and that we do not face a Russian Century, but this paper has tried to suggest that the problems of Europe are highly complex and that they cannot be solved by mere wishful thinking.

THE REVOLUTION OF 1848

LORD ELTON

Godfrey, Lord Elton, a Fellow of Queen's College, Oxford, and a Lecturer in Modern History from 1919 to 1939, is at present secretary of the Rhodes Trust. He has been active in politics, serving for a time as a Labor member of Parliament, and has written a number of scholarly works. In his book, *The Revolutionary Idea in France,* first published in 1923 and reprinted several times since, Lord Elton traces the continuing revolutionary elements in French political history from the Great Revolution of 1789 to the founding of the Third Republic in an attempt to establish the basis for a scientific study of revolutionary phenomena. With generous quotations from Alexis de Tocqueville, the perceptive observer and analyst of political institutions who participated in the 1848 movement, Lord Elton, in the excerpt printed below, endeavors to show that 1848 was a "new" revolution in France—"the economic revolution" —aiming primarily at a redistribution of wealth.

I HAVE tried to disentangle and summarily to present the three constituents of the Revolution of 1848: the universal dissatisfaction with the ingloriousness and corruption of the July monarchy; the movement for the Republic as the logical completion of the first Revolution; and, lastly, the new Revolutionary socialism. We shall find each playing its appointed part in the Revolution itself.

On the first day (February 22nd) the pervading discontent takes shape in vague disturbance which, on the second, defines itself as the successful insurrection against Guizot, his system and its results. This is the *first phase* (Feb. 22, 23).

The *second phase* is equally brief (Feb. 24–26). On the third day (February 24th) the Reform Party finds to its consternation that the Revolution is not over. The Republicans have taken it in hand. Louis Philippe abdicates; a provisional government is acclaimed and proclaims the Republic.

The *third phase* is the struggle between the rival policies within the successful Republican party. On one side the Republicans-and-no-more for whom the Revolution had achieved its purpose when it proclaimed the Republic, the logical completion of the Revolution of 1789. The tricolour was their flag. On the other side those for whom the end of monarchy was no more than the inevitable preliminary to a profounder modification of society in the interests of the working man, the economic Revolution. Their emblem was the red flag. The struggle does not end until the Havenots of the new Revolution are finally defeated by the Haves of the old in the bloody street fighting of June 24–26. Here — as the peasants pour in from the country to defend, together with their middle class co-heirs, the legacy of 1789 — Paris is for the first time defeated by France, a fact of immense importance. At this point then the new Revolution is driven underground, to await further remarkable destinies.

From Lord Elton, *The Revolutionary Idea in France, 1789–1871* (2nd edn., London, 1931), pp. 132–148. By permission of Edward Arnold (Publishers) Ltd.

Such was the Revolution of 1848 in brief. We will examine it in some detail, for invaluable to the students of revolutions is a revolution so compact, so brief, in many ways so typical. Moreover, among the contemporary records, besides the picturesque autobiographies, miscalled histories, of Louis Blanc and Lamartine, we possess in de Tocqueville's *Souvenirs* the evidence of an eye-witness of genius, himself the first and greatest student of revolutions.

First comes the Reform insurrection of February 22nd and 23rd. The political banquets, which the ministry of Guizot had forbidden, were the immediate occasion, but by no means the cause, of the Revolution. It was tacitly understood that the opposition would hold one last banquet, and that the government without obstructing it would charge its promoters in the courts, with whom the verdict would rest: that is all. On the 20th February almost all the opposition journals published an appeal to Paris at large to join in an immense demonstration on the day of the banquet; the National Guard itself was included in the invitation. The government at once forbade the banquet, and announced that it would take steps to prevent it by force. The 22nd was the appointed day. There were crowds in the streets, uneasy but purposeless crowds which thronged past the Madeleine, crossed that great central scene of so much bloodshedding which Parisians have named the Place of Concord, and so over the Pont Royale to the Chamber of Deputies. There they were dispersed without loss of life by a regiment of dragoons. De Tocqueville dined that night with a fellow-deputy. Twenty places were laid, but only five guests sat down to dinner. The five, he says, were "pensive." On his way home he may have noticed the distant flicker of the flames in which street-urchins were burning some of the benches in the Champs Elysées. Lamartine, at least, observed them thoughtfully.

At dawn, on the 23rd, troops occupied the principal posts of vantage in Paris, and there awaited events, extremely cold and uncomfortable. Few people were to be seen about, only an occasional burst of distant firing echoed mysteriously from the labyrinth of streets in the neighbourhood of the Hotel de Ville. In the evening, however, a large crowd encountered a regiment of the line before the Ministry of Foreign Affairs, was fired on by some misunderstanding, and took to its heels, leaving a number of dead. Later that night the corpses were placed on a bier and borne processionally by torchlight through the streets. "The government is massacring the people," sobbed de Tocqueville's cook next morning. And through the night armed men went from house to house, barricades were hastily put up, and the church bells rang to summon Paris to further insurrection. Louis Philippe could hear them distinctly from the Tuileries. During that night he invited Thiers, leader of the opposition, to form a government. The Reform-rebellion was over. Early in the morning of the twenty-fourth he lay down for a few hours, fully dressed. He could hear, where he lay, the confused murmur of conversation among his counsellors in an adjacent room, and beyond it the sounds of a distant but recurrent fusillade.

There had been an odd effect of discipline about the two columns which were the nucleus of the crowd which had got itself "massacred" this night of the twenty-third. They had seemed to be in no doubt about their objects or their route, these men, and to recognise officers from whom they received orders, and at least once a purposeful little band had detached itself from the main column and disappeared unostentatiously down a side street upon an unknown mission.

This nucleus was drawn, no doubt, from the secret societies which, in increasing numbers since 1830, had been giving shelter to illegal opinions. Louis Blanc gives an interesting picture, in the introduction to the *Histoire de dix ans,* of the French Carbonari under the Restoration drilling on straw in empty houses. The *Droits de l'homme,* the *Famille,* the *Saisons* — all preserved the republican and revolutionary traditions, and, as we have seen, to these since 1830 had been adding itself the new revolutionary economic gospel. The secret societies were often divided into sections of twenty members, each with an officer and under-officer. (Thus, for example, the *Droits de l'homme.*) And hence no doubt the all but military discipline in portions of the crowds of 1848. All these societies, too, had had experience in one or other of the insurrections of 1832, 1834, and 1839. But it must be recognised that it was these societies which were created by the requirements of forbidden revolutionary opinion, not the opinion which was created by the societies. Nor must the importance of the secret societies even in this merely Parisian Revolution be exaggerated. Lamartine, who was in as good a position as anyone to estimate their influence, observed that "the very limited effects which can be produced by a conspirator . . . are influential only when they serve a general idea or a pre-existing passion. . . . In the modern state the only all-powerful conspirator is public opinion."

This insurrection of the twenty-second and twenty-third had been the work of the party of reform; *à bas Guizot* had been its rallying-cry. It had been successful, and there had even been illuminations at night. The second insurrection developed out of it early on the twenty-fourth. The troops proved reluctant to take the offensive against it, and Thiers ordered them to withdraw on the Tuileries and sent his colleague — Barrot — to announce to the crowds the concessions extorted from the king. He himself within a few hours was to be slinking homewards *incognito* and by devious routes, shaken by hysterical sobs, muttering incoherently to himself and incontinently turning tail at the first hint of a crowd — even of street-urchins. The Palais-Royal, original home of the house of Orleans, was captured and pillaged. Louis Philippe, attempting to rouse the enthusiasm of the National Guard, was received with chilling

indifference, lost heart and abdicated in favour of the Comte de Paris, his grandson. That afternoon the crowd destroyed the throne in the Tuileries. The Chamber of Deputies, which had proclaimed the Comte de Paris king and his mother regent, was invaded, the Republic was proclaimed and the republican members of the Chamber announced amidst uproar the members of a provisional government selected by the staff of the National Guard. These made their way across the tumult of Paris to the Hotel de Ville, where they had to effect a sort of coalition with the government already selected by the *Reforme.*

On the twenty-sixth the Provisional Coalition Government proclaimed the Republic. Once more France was to receive a Revolution ready made from Paris. The Provisional Government had indeed some misgivings in this matter; its first draft of the proclamation stated that *neither the people of Paris nor the Provisional Government pretend to substitute their opinion for the opinion of the citizens, who will be consulted as to the final form of the Government.* Lamartine asserts that in one of his many addresses to the mob in the streets at this time, speaking of the proposed Republic, he said, "We have only one right, that of proclaiming . . . our own will, as the people of Paris . . . leaving to the country and its thirty-six millions who are not present and have the same right as ourselves . . . the expression of their sovereign will by means of universal suffrage . . . the one foundation of any national republic." The people shouted in reply, "Yes, yes. France is not here. Paris is the head, but Paris must guide, and not tyrannise over, the body." Thus remote was the populace for the moment from the Jacobin view of the relation of Paris to France. A later draft of the proclamation was less apologetic: *The Provisional Government wills the Republic, under condition of approval by the people, who will be immediately consulted.* And in the final announcement of the 26th the Provisional Government appeared to have overcome its scruples: *In*

the name of the French people, Monarchy,
under every form, is abolished without pos-
sibility of return. Without possibility of
return! Thus had the men of 1789 abolished
the Bourbon monarchy and the restored
Bourbon monarchy the empire of Napoleon.

The Provisional Government had now
achieved the only task on which it was
agreed. It had no recognisable mandate, no
instruments save what it could improvise
and no authority save what it could usurp.
And from now onwards it carried disruption in its heart.

The third, last, and longest phase of
the Revolution is occupied by the conflict
between the warring principles within the
Provisional and Coalition Government.
The issue between them is clear. The
Republicans of the old Revolution (Lamartine and five others) were for the Republic,
the democracy of universal suffrage and
no more. The new revolutionaries (Louis
Blanc, Albert, Flocon) were for carrying
out the further, economic Revolution, without waiting for the verdict of the nation.
The instincts of Jacobinism were reviving
rapidly indeed. And at the moment the
new revolutionaries wielded the same formidable weapon as the men of 1793, an
armed body of supporters in the streets,
organised, not now in the Jacobin clubs,
but in the *Société républicaine centrale* of
Blanqui and the *Club de la Révolution* of
Barbès. For some days no soldiers, no police
were to be seen about the streets; "the
people alone carried arms, kept watch over
public places, was on guard, issued orders,
and awarded punishments."

But in spite of this resumption of tradition there is a new and quite unmistakable
tang of modernity about this Revolution.
Thus de Tocqueville observed "a very general effort to placate the new master. Great
landowners liked to recall that they had
always been hostile to the bourgeois class
and favourable to the people: and the
bourgeois themselves remembered with a
certain pride how their fathers had been
workmen, and when, owing to the inevitable obscurity of genealogies, they could

not trace themselves back to a workman
who had actually worked with his hands,
they would at least attempt to descend from
a ne'er-do-well who had made his fortune
for himself. In fact the desire for the
publicity of such details was as great as a
little while ago it would have been for their
concealment." And "just now everyone did
his best to make what he could out of
any black sheep the family possessed. Any
cousin, or brother or son one might be
lucky enough to own who had ruined himself by his excesses was well on the way to
succeed; while if he had contrived to win
notoriety by some extravagant theory or
other there was no height to which he
might not aspire. The majority of the com-
missaries and sub-commissaries of the government were persons of this sort." The
Duc de Broglie, poor gentleman, daily
expected the collapse of civilisation.

The clubs began to establish their dictatorship at once. Even on February 25th
an armed workman, spokesman of an immense crowd, demanded the *right to work*
(*droit au travail*), Louis Blanc's phrase.
Next day the establishment of *national*
workshops was decreed.

On February 28th another organised
demonstration demanded a Ministry of
Progress. It carried banners on which were
the words *Organisation du travail*, a phrase
again of Louis Blanc's, and Louis Blanc
himself supported the demand, and succeeded in persuading the government to
create a Workers' Commission. Louis Blanc
and Albert took up their quarters in the
Luxemburg, whither they summoned representatives of various trades. And there
this Commission decreed the reduction of
the working day from eleven to ten hours
in Paris, from twelve to eleven in the
provinces. Such were the not very formidable first-fruits of Louis Blanc's "perilous
chimera." The employers, however, paid
remarkably little attention to the modest
manifesto, and the Luxemburg Commission, which was permitted neither authority
nor money, could scarcely enforce it.

For the third time, on March 17th, the

clubs organised a *journée;* this time to exact the postponement for a fortnight of the election of the Assembly which was to supersede the Provisional Government. In this singularly short interval the country was to be converted to socialism. For the third time, and the last, the clubs were successful. On this occasion Blanqui (director of the *Société républicaine centrale*) was spokesman. "His speech amounted," says Lamartine, "to a demand for the implicit obedience of the government to the dictatorship of the mob as expressed by the clubs." For Jacobinism, in fact.

On April 16th there was yet another effort, and it failed: the bourgeois members of the National Guard lined up before the Hotel de Ville with cries of "Down with the communists!" The clubs had more than half Paris against them and the whole of France.

Meanwhile the government was experimenting with "national workshops." These were not organised by Louis Blanc, neither did they resemble the "social workshops" suggested in *L'Organisation du Travail.* The members did not work at their own craft, but were regimented into brigades which were set to level the Champs de Mars at two francs a day (and, later, one franc when there was no work), a system ruinous to the exchequer and humiliating to the worker. Unemployment growing continually, the numbers in the *ateliers nationaux* rose from 6,000 in March to 100,000 in May; many of them were artists, actors, men of letters, clerks and the like. The government, which was responsible for their distress, was in fact distributing charitable relief under a not very convincing disguise. The *ateliers nationaux,* thinks Lamartine, were a guarantee against disorder and socialism. "They counterbalanced," he says, "the Luxemburg commission and the clubs, and on several occasions saved Paris, though Paris did not know." They became "seditious" themselves only with the arrival of the Assembly in Paris and its plan for their own dissolution. Clearly this was an expedient, not a system; and clearly

the *ateliers nationaux* (where, whatever their own skilled craft, men worked all together at the same unskilled labour) were notably unlike the *ateliers sociaux* of Louis Blanc, to whom a remarkable historical perversion has sometimes attributed them. "Directed and controlled by leaders who shared the secret views of the anti-socialist members of the government," says Lamartine of the experiment of 1848, "they were instinct with the spirit of Louis Blanc's adversaries." The failures of 1848 are no reflection upon socialist theory, for the socialists were never in control even of the Provisional Government, and with the advent of the Constituent Assembly elected by universal suffrage they became impotent.

The Assembly met on May 4th. Universal suffrage had given an overwhelming majority to the possessing classes, and in an overwhelming majority the Assembly approved the anti-socialist Republic. Only one or two of the new revolutionaries sat in the Assembly, and the executive commission of five which it appointed and which was to name the ministers was hostile to them. The clubs remained the stronghold of the new Revolution. It was clear that there would soon be conflict once again, and perhaps mortal conflict, between this Paris of the clubs and France. In 1793 we saw Paris dictatress of a powerless and not very resentful France. In 1830 too, although a group of provincial deputies speedily assumed control of it, the Revolution was Paris-made. But in 1848 France was becoming consciously restive beneath the yoke of her feverish capital.

De Tocqueville, in his provincial constituency, at the time of the elections for the Constituent Assembly of 1848, observed this new impatience at close quarters. "For the first time," he says, "Paris inspired universal hatred as well as universal terror. In France the attitude of the provincials towards Paris and the central authority of which it is the seat is very much like that of the English towards their aristocracy, which they view sometimes with impatience and often with jealousy, but which in their hearts they love because they always hope to employ its privileges for their own ends. Now, however, Paris and those who spoke in her name had so misused their power and seemed to take the rest of the country into so little account, that the idea of shaking off the yoke and at last achieving independence presented itself to many minds which had never dreamt of such a thing before."

And in 1848 France was an altogether more formidable rival than in 1793 or 1830. The extension of the telegraph was beginning to make her *aware*. The violent decisions of Paris no longer came to her belated and irreparable: she was growing into an organic and self-conscious whole. But if the telegraph had given her consciousness, the more recent development of the railway had given her *power*. The deputies who upheld her majesty would no longer be left defenceless to the street insurrections of Paris. When de Tocqueville set out for Paris his constituents bade him farewell with tears in their eyes, "for it was generally believed in the provinces that the deputies would be exposed to great danger in Paris, and several of the good folk said to me, 'If the National Assembly is attacked we will come and defend you.'"

And lastly, besides being more conscious and more formidable, the provinces had in 1848 a very particular quarrel with their capital. As we have seen, in Paris in 1848 a violent minority once more attempted to impose its will upon the country; and this will was not, as in 1793, the national will for victory concentrated in a class but the will of a class for its own advancement. This class, as we saw, found no place in a society which had been remoulded and had hardened into its new shape before the existence in it of a new element had been suspected. Not participating in the legacy of the Revolution of 1789, that class desired a Revolution of its own, the economic Revolution of the Have-nots against the Haves: of the excluded, against the heirs, of 1789. Unfortunately for the new revolutionaries the land settlement of the old

Revolution, by parcelling out the soil of France in infinite sub-division, had included among the possessing class the vast majority of the nation; and though these peasants owned little, those who own least are usually the most tenacious of their property. Hence the sinister news of the designs upon property did not, like English Chartism, alarm the middle classes only, but united provincial France in one compact brotherhood against the half of Paris. Here and there in the towns the industrial workers espoused the new Revolution. But France outside her cities was of one mind: in face of the threat to property all classes and parties drew instinctively together. "Property . . . had become a sort of brotherhood. Rich . . . and poor . . . all held themselves brothers and all were equally concerned to defend the common heritage." Such was the mind of provincial France on May 4th at the time of the meeting of the National Constituent Assembly, to which it had returned so great a majority against the new Revolution. In less than two months it was to be at death grips with the new principle in the streets of Paris.

During those few intervening weeks Paris saw again the tactics of Jacobinism. It was argued daily in the clubs, notes de Tocqueville, that "the people is always superior to its delegates, and never completely resigns its will into their hands. A principle true enough, from which, however, was drawn the false consequence that the workmen of Paris *were* the people of France." This was the principle put into practice upon May 15th, when an immense crowd invaded the Assembly, and amidst uproar and confusion declared the Assembly dissolved and proclaimed a Socialist Provisional Government. The National Guard arrived not a moment too soon and dispersed the demonstrators in inglorious flight. De Tocqueville's recollections of the whole amazing scene should be studied carefully by anyone interested in the psychology of crowds.

Six days later was held a Feast of Concord; a manifestation of fraternity at which three hundred thousand armed men, carrying the rifles with which they were to shoot each other down next month, defiled past a platform on which were seated the members of the National Assembly each with a pistol, a life-preserver, or a dagger concealed about his person. The official programme enjoined "fraternal confusion," and the confusion at least was unmistakable.

By now civil war was in the air. Sooner or later Haves and Have-nots must come to grips. And inevitably it was upon the *ateliers nationaux* that the issue was joined. The Assembly was determined to dissolve this vast camp of over a hundred thousand armed and discontented workmen. These were still employed, humiliatingly and unproductively, upon levelling the Champ de Mars. "It is not our will to work that is lacking," they protested, "but useful work suited to our callings"; and they refused to disband. Fighting began on June 24th. The workmen fought without leaders, but with the utmost resolution. Never before or since have they struggled with such good hope. For a victory in Paris might give them France, and the socialist theories being in their heyday still it seemed to them that victory would be followed by the millennium. But the very ferocity of the insurrection was fatal to it: for the possessing classes could not help but realise that either it must be crushed, or the society they knew destroyed. And consequently they, too, left their houses and fought desperately. For both sides it was victory or slavery.

And for the first time France intervened. Already on the 25th by every road not actually held by insurgents, the possessing classes, noble and peasant alike, were pouring into Paris. By the 26th they were coming from five hundred miles away; and while the insurgents had no reserves, the defence could draw upon the whole of France. France had defeated Paris, and this defeat profoundly modified the form taken by the revolutionary idea when it next emerged, in the Commune of 1871. For the first time the whole was able to impose its will upon the part: a fact of tremendous

significance. Perhaps never again — consider this — will a minority carry a revolution to success, at least by way of insurrection. In this year a page is turned in the history of revolutions, *and conceivably the last*.

In this conflict one bond had held together the defence, one interest it shared in common — property. An aged kinsman of de Tocqueville's refused to leave the fighting. "What would these brave folk say if I left them?" he replied, pointing to his heterogeneous comrades in arms. "They know that I have much more to lose than they if the insurrection triumphs." By the 26th the victory had been won. Of the prisoners the majority were shot out of hand or transported *en masse* without trial. In less than six months Louis Napoleon was Prince President of the Republic.

The new and short-lived constitution of 1848 had asserted, together with the classic dogma of the separation of powers, that "all power emanates from the people." The legislature was an assembly of 750 elected by universal suffrage (for the first time the Revolution was completely justifying the Declaration of Rights of 1789); the executive was a President to hold office for four years, choosing its own ministers. Who was to elect the President? If the Assembly, it would elect Cavaignac. But if the people? Lamartine knew that he would not be elected by the Assembly. "Let God and the people pronounce," he said. "Something must be left to Providence." God and the people, he hoped, would pronounce in favour of himself. By December, 1848, however, the people at least had decided for a man with unusually short legs and a face like a fish. Once more the Revolution was about to hand itself over to a despot.

It is instructive to note, in this matter of electing the President, the completely divergent wills of the people and their representatives. By orthodox theory the will of the Assembly was the will of France, and the Assembly would have chosen Cavaignac. Twice already, however, in 1793 as well as in 1848, we have seen the Paris streets claiming to speak for France:

they would have chosen Ledru-Rollin. And France did in fact choose Louis Napoleon. Each of the three "Frances" would have spoken differently. The truth is that the Assembly had been elected for a definite purpose, to protect the principle of property against Paris, and, this duty once discharged, its will bore no relation to the will of its constituents. This was in Louis Napoleon's mind when, preluding despotism, he invited its successor, the Legislature, to "associate itself with the national will of which his own election had been the expression." This justification he had too for the appeal by plebiscite to France. Since, however, the plebiscite was preceded by a bloody and treacherous *coup d'état,* and accompanied by about ten thousand transportations, the justification was morally of the slenderest.

Plebiscite accepted both the *coup d'état* of December, 1851, and the assumption of the imperial title a year later (December, 1852). For a second time the Revolution of 1789 had surrendered to Caesar. And in return for what? The first Empire, we have seen, while destroying the form, preserved the substance of the first Revolution; and the second Empire too, while destroying the form, undertook to preserve the essentials of the substance. The distinction is that the first Napoleon was needed to guarantee and protect the achievement of a vast movement of the human spirit in its creative phase; the second Napoleon came to defend in a movement static now and not creative that part of its achievement which it could not be cajoled into bartering away. The first was a task for genius, the second for cunning.

But if Louis Napoleon stood for the preservation of the old Revolution he stood for the destruction of the new. In the eyes of the middle classes and peasants he guaranteed property against the *Rouges* who, after the disaster of 1848, were believed to be plotting a second rising for 1852. Once more Empire was welcomed because it promised *Order.* And if the name Napoleon spelt Order it spelt *Glory* too. Of the hundreds of thousands of peasants who voted for that name not a few supposed themselves to be voting for the "Little Corporal" himself. After more than three decades in which to weary of weakness and humiliation, France was heartsick for the Napoleonic touch. Glory, as we saw, had been the one desire common to all parties in the Revolution of 1848: Order had become an even more urgent need in face of the threat of the new revolutionaries to society as constituted by the old. In return for security for these two chief elements in the substance of the old revolution, France was prepared to forego the third, Equality, and, a little less readily, since the loss was more apparent and immediate, the form, the Republic. Thus it was the New Revolution which yielded to Louis Napoleon, and this was the element in the Revolution of 1848 which failed. The old Revolution welcomed him as protector of its tradition, and the Revolution of 1848 in so far as it desired no more than Glory, and then Order, may be said to have succeeded. And thus Napoleon the third, like Napoleon the first, was demanded by the needs of a Revolution; he was less urgently demanded, less the inevitable, because the forces which called for him were spent. . . .

THE SECOND REPUBLIC

J. P. T. BURY

A Fellow of Corpus Christi College, Cambridge, J. P. T. Bury is an expert on modern French history. In his historical survey, *France, 1814–1940,* he restricted himself to a straightforward narrative account, emphasizing accuracy of information rather than attempting to prove a thesis. However, in the following excerpt dealing with the revolution of 1848, Bury departs from this standard of pure objectivity and ventures some moderate judgments. This represents a different view from that provided by Elton, for Bury tends to subordinate the social and economic revolution which forms the basis for Elton's interpretation.

THE PROCLAMATION of a Republic in Paris evoked an extraordinary variety and intensity of emotion both in France and throughout Europe, emotion which ranged from the deepest alarm and anxiety to the most extravagant hopefulness and enthusiasm. The young Prince de Broglie, then a diplomat in Rome, was one of those who heard the news with alarm: "Country, family, honour," he wrote later, "ambition, interests, personal security — all seemed to be threatened at once and to fall engulfed in the same abyss. Men could think only of 1793. The Republic meant bloodshed, confiscation, terror and war." All those who had possessions were indeed anxious. Within a week, more than 1,300 English people had hurried home. Business, already slack, came almost to a standstill; unemployment increased and there were outbreaks of machine smashing. Stocks fell; rich people sold their effects, while at the same time there was a run upon banks, many of which were obliged to suspend payment; even the gold reserve in the Bank of France sank to such a low level that on March 1st, 1848, dealings in paper money had to be stopped. This was one side of the picture, the gloomy side. On the other we see an extraordinary Romantic ebullience and optimism which manifested themselves in many ways: in the sudden efflorescence of clubs — no less than 450 appeared within a month in Paris and its suburbs, clubs with names that echoed those of the Great Revolution, clubs of Jacobins and Montagnards, and clubs for the emancipation of European peoples or of the feminine sex; in an abundance of banquets, banquets of "the Federation of European Peoples," of the "Friends of Poland," of "Democratic Women," of "Les travailleurs de la pensée" and a hundred more, banquets which always ended with some resounding toast — "To the Mountain of 1793" — "To Mistrust, sister of Vigilance" — "To Jesus Christ" — "To democratic Germany" — "To Jean-Jacques Rousseau" — "To the oppressed peoples" — and to many others; in the spate of newspapers and pamphlets which poured forth as soon as the new rulers abolished the stamp duty and removed the restrictions imposed by the law of 1835 on the liberty of the Press, papers and pamphlets which abounded not with news but with social and political programmes and doc-

From J. P. T. Bury, *France, 1814–1940* (Philadelphia, 1949), pp. 72–81. By permission of the University of Pennsylvania Press.

17

trinaire declarations; in the planting of Trees of Liberty and their blessing by the clergy — for the Church, too, had been swept by liberal enthusiasms since the election in 1846 of a Liberal Pope; and in the grandiloquent language of the new Government itself, as instanced by the opening words of the preamble to its proclamation of February 26th announcing its intention to abolish the death penalty: "The Provisional Government, convinced that generosity is the supreme part of policy and that each revolution effected by the French people owes it to the world to consecrate yet one more philosophic truth, considering that there is no principle more sublime than that of the inviolability of human life; considering that, in the memorable days in which we are living, not a cry of vengeance has arisen from the mouth of the people. . . ." In short, among the people, the *gens du peuple* of Paris, the Revolution was hailed as the dawn of a new era. It was not long before their hopes were to be bitterly disappointed.

In many ways the consummation of the Revolution recalled that of 1830. Once again journalists played a great part, once again rival sets of insurgents bid against one another for power; once again the Hôtel de Ville was a place of decisive importance for determining the nature of the new Government; once again the period of unrest and popular demonstrations continued long after the Revolution itself was over; and once again there were two conflicting views of the object of the Revolution, each of which had its supporters within the Government itself. Accordingly, this Provisional Government which emerged represented a compromise. All its members save one, Albert, a workman, included in recognition of the part played by the people in the Revolution, were of bourgeois origin, more or less well-known Republicans, for the most part lawyers, orators and journalists by profession. On the one hand there were the men of the newspaper, *Le National,* people like Arago, Crémieux, Marie, Garnier-Pagès and Lamartine, for

Lamartine had more or less abandoned poetry for politics and now became Minister for Foreign Affairs; on the other it included the men who supported the rival paper, *La Réforme,* such as Louis Blanc, Albert, Flocon and Ledru-Rollin. For the former the Revolution was a political event: it means the completion of the political work of the Great Revolution by the substitution of a free and democratic Republic based upon universal male suffrage for a monarchy based upon a restricted franchise: but for the men of the *Réforme* it implied a social and economic as well as a political transformation, and in Louis Blanc, the author of *L'Organisation du Travail,* they had a social observer who was acutely aware of the evils of the new industrial age and who was most eager to abolish them. The great drama of 1848 lies in the conflict between those who want to seize the opportunity to solve the social problem by radical reforms of the conditions of labour and those who are determined to resist social changes which they fear will lead to chaos and anarchy. And herein also lies the great contrast between 1830 and 1848: in 1830 the middle classes were undisputed victors, in 1848 they are for a while on the defensive.

The men of the *Réforme* were a minority in the Provisional Government, but they had sufficient influence and sufficient popular backing to make themselves felt at the outset. On the 25th February only the eloquence of Lamartine saved the tricolour from being displaced by the Socialist red flag; this was symbolic of the conflict between the old and the new revolutionaries — but, if the Government compromised by allowing a red rosette to be affixed to the standard of the tricolour, they had to make more conspicuous concessions to the demand for social reform when they reduced daily working hours to ten in Paris and eleven in the provinces and when they issued a proclamation recognizing the right to work. Moreover, although they refused the request for the establishment of a separate Ministry of Labour, they set up a permanent commission which was to sit at the Luxembourg Palace and examine labour problems under the presidency of Louis Blanc. Finally, in order to deal with the acute problem of Parisian unemployment, they created National Workshops. All this marked a radical departure from the *laissez-faire* attitude of the July Monarchy. The Government for the first time in French history were ready to guarantee work and to set about the task of organizing labour; but their organization of labour in the National Workshops was to be a parody of the "Organisation du Travail" envisaged by Louis Blanc. None the less, these first social successes were sufficient to confirm the hopes of the enthusiastic workers. Was not one of their own kind, Albert, in the Government? Was not Louis Blanc in charge of labour questions? Was not George Sand who had echoed his charitable formula "To each according to his needs," busy helping the new ministers draft their decrees? And if the Government had not yet abolished the work-book or done away with the Combination Laws, had it not guaranteed the right to work? All these considerations appeared signs of still better things to come and were hailed by many as a mere prelude to the complete transformation of society. But the fact that some of these social measures were extorted more or less under pressure by armed demonstrators had been enough to alarm both the moderates in the Government and most of their sympathizers outside it. The political course of the Revolution was soon to give the moderates and conservatives, the forces of order, the defenders of the existing society, an opportunity to rally and eventually to go over to the offensive.

After abolishing "monarchy of every kind without possibility of return" and removing stamp duties and many other restrictions on the liberty of the citizen, the Provisional Government had hastened to arrange for the establishment of the Republic on a regular basis. Accordingly, on March 5th, they decreed that elections to a National Constituent Assembly should be held on April 9th and that every Frenchman over twenty-one years of age should be entitled to a vote. Thus, by a stroke of the pen, universal male suffrage was introduced into France and the electorate was increased from some 200,000 to some 9,000,000. Moreover, in spite of the elementary education bill of 1833 and the growth of the popular press to which we referred in the last chapter, the majority of this vast new electorate was still illiterate. In his *Les Paysans,* written in 1845, Balzac has a striking passage on the meaning of legislation for the provinces: "For twenty million beings in France the law is merely a piece of white paper stuck on the door of the Church or the Town Hall (Mairie). . . . Many mayors of cantons turn their copies of the *Bulletin des Lois* into bags for holding raisins and seeds. As for the mere mayors of communes you would be shocked by the number who cannot read or write and by the way in which the civil registers are kept." If such were the mayors, it is clear that the ordinary peasant or worker was unlikely to be more lettered. In these circumstances, although the Republic was giving them the vote, it was not at all certain that their vote would be for the Republic. Blanqui indeed had at once seen that if elections were held quickly they would be likely to produce conservative results, and Ledru-Rollin as Minister of the Interior, did his best to educate the new electors and secure an Assembly "animated by a revolutionary spirit" by sending out special "Commissioners of the Republic" to all the departments. But the Government would only consent to postpone the elections for a fortnight and meanwhile events in Paris and various parts of the country served but to increase the moderates' distrust of the Republic and its capacity to maintain order. Thus the postponement of the elections was itself extracted from the Government by outside pressure. On the 16th March the bourgeois National Guards of the western districts of Paris had demonstrated against a measure dissolving some of their companies: on the following day Clubs and crowds from the east had penetrated into the Hôtel de Ville and compelled the Government to postpone the general elections. On the 21st a Radical Republican "Club of Clubs" was founded which opened branches in the provinces and associated itself with Ledru-Rollin in his attempt to republicanize the electorate. On the 9th April another club, in which Armand Barbès was a prominent figure, called upon the Government to take over the Bank of France and to nationalize the insurance companies, railways, mines and salt works and canals; and on the 16th there was a workers' demonstration in favour of a further postponement of the elections, which alarmed the Government so much that they summoned the National Guard to their aid. Meanwhile in many country districts also the Revolution had been a signal for disturbances, for attacks on Jews and forest guards, and on justices of the peace, who were responsible for the collection of the unpopular *droits réunis* tax. The tales of these disturbances, of Paris disorder and of Socialist threats to property soon spread to the remotest parts of the country and naturally were not diminished in retelling. Furthermore, the Provisional Government had found themselves in financial difficulties which had led them as early as March 16th to add an additional forty-five centimes to direct taxation. This was a measure which inevitably made them unpopular with a thrifty peasantry already alarmed by rumours of disorder. In fact, the difference between 1789 and 1848 was very marked, in spite of the conscious echoes of the Great Revolution which resounded in the clubs. In 1789 the great mass of the nation, the country dwellers as well as the bourgeoisie, had been eager for the abolition of feudal privileges and political inequality: but in 1848 the number of Frenchmen who genuinely desired a social revolution and the abolition of economic inequality was comparatively small. The peasantry, so many of them now proprietors, were only scared by the stories of the Parisian Socialists and their rumoured

talk of redistributing or doing away with individual property by some new agrarian law. And so when election day came and eighty-four per cent of the electorate went to the polls, most of them for the first time and village folk often headed by their parish priests as they marched to the booths, the votes cast were above all votes for order. In other words, the result of the elections was a crushing defeat for the extreme Radicals and Socialists, who won only 100 out of 876 seats.

The new Assembly, which thus comprised a large majority of moderate Republicans, former Orleanists, and Legitimists, was bound to come sooner or later into conflict with the extremists who were still able to exercise great influence in Paris. A few days after it met in May the Provisional Government resigned their power and the executive authority was entrusted to a so-called Executive Commission which included several members of the late Government, but not Louis Blanc or Albert. Already the Assembly was beginning to show its Conservative tendencies, and on the 12th May there took place the first of a series of demonstrations against it which culminated in one on the 15th when the Palais Bourbon was invaded by a mob, a club orator pronounced the Assembly's dissolution, and most of the crowd, headed by Barbès and Albert, then proceeded to the Hôtel de Ville to concoct a new Government. But the National Guard rallied and the newly raised Mobile Guards cleared the Assembly. The Hôtel de Ville was re-occupied and many of the leaders of this attempt at a second Revolution including Barbès, Blanqui and Albert, were arrested and prosecuted. The apostles of a Social Republic had, as George Sand perceived, committed a moral as well as a political blunder: "They had without serious cause . . . given the signal for a rising against the law of the Republic; they had thrown people into a permanent state of anxiety and in some sort justified future *coups de force!*"

Meanwhile labour problems again came to the fore. In the Assembly on May 10th

Louis Blanc once again proposed the creation of a Ministry of Labour and Progress, but the Assembly contented itself with setting up a committee which was to conduct inquiry into labour conditions in agriculture and industry, canton by canton, throughout the country. It was optimistic enough to hope that the inquiry would be completed in a few weeks, but such a vast operation in unquiet times was bound to be protracted, and in fact it was to continue into 1850. A special problem was, however, presented by the National Workshops in Paris. In his *Organisation du Travail* Louis Blanc had conceived of National Workshops as a means of combating unemployment and utilizing skilled labour in an orderly fashion under State direction. But the Workshops of Paris in 1848, as they were organized under the direction of Marie and Thomas, were a travesty of Louis Blanc's conception and were like nothing so much as the *ateliers de charité* of the Ancien Régime. They had been set up too hastily, under revolutionary pressure and without adequate administrative services to control them, with the result that some 50,000 workmen had soon been enrolled when there was real work for only 10,000. The remainder had to be occupied and were therefore employed on tasks such as levelling the Champ de Mars for two francs a day, work of such little value that, as someone said, they might just as well have spent their time in bottling the waters of the Seine. The presence of such a large body of men doing such unprofitable work was soon recognized by the Government as demoralizing for the men themselves, a drain on public funds, a danger to public order (many of the workers having taken part in the disturbances of May 15th) and in consequence an impediment to the recovery of business; and so it was decided that, after a census had been taken, the Workshops should be dissolved, that bachelors between eighteen and twenty-five should have the choice of dismissal or enrolment in the army; and that the rest should either accept what work could be offered by private employers or be sent to work on public enterprises in the provinces. After some delay the Assembly passed a decree on these lines and towards the end of June the Executive Commission of the Government decided to proceed immediately with the dissolution of the Workshops.

The result was infinitely tragic. When once they heard of the decision the workers were furious at what they regarded as the Government's and Assembly's treachery in going back on the guarantee of the right to work. The persistence of the economic crisis, in spite of the rule of a Republican régime, had steadily hardened social antagonisms, making the employers sterner in their resolve to end what they regarded as social anarchy and the young workers all the more bitter at the choice now presented to them between conscription and unemployment. And so the men of the National Workshops, and the unemployed who had been refused admission to them, determined to resist the order for dissolution, and all the working-class quarters of Paris rose in sympathy with them. For a second time within a few months Paris saw the barricades go up. No persuasion could induce the men to disperse peaceably and on June 24th, 1848, the Assembly gave General Cavaignac the title of Chief of the Executive Power with full authority to use force. Reinforcement of troops, for the first time in French history, were hurried to the city by train, and three days of bitter fighting ensued. It was a remarkable insurrection — not led by any of the Socialist chiefs or deputies, but, in Tocqueville's words, one in which 100,000 insurgents fought "without a war-cry, without chiefs, or a standard, and yet with a cohesion and a military skill which surprised the oldest officers." It was "not the work of a group of conspirators, but the rising of one part of the population against the other. Women took part in it as much as men . . . they hoped for victory to ease the lot of their husbands, and help to bring up their children." "It was not a political struggle . . . but class war, a kind of slave-war." As such it had all the ruthlessness of class or slave warfare, and was bitterly fought, and ruthlessly suppressed. Many were killed, 15,000 people were arrested and 4,000 deported, mostly to Algeria. All Socialists were now under suspicion and Louis Blanc hurriedly took refuge in England. Clubs were placed under supervision. New press laws were introduced, reimposing a cautionary payment on those who wished to publish newspapers and making attacks upon certain institutions indictable offences. In September the working day in Paris was once again increased to twelve hours and in many instances in the years to follow it became still longer. When the Assembly applauded Cavaignac for his achievement in suppressing the insurrection Lamartine exclaimed: "The Republic is dead." When Lamennais was obliged by the new press laws to cease publishing his paper Le Peuple Constituant he did so with the bitter words "Silence to the poor man," and commented that the spectacle presented by France after the June Days was not that of Republican France but of the "saturnalia of reaction around its bloodstained tomb." The forces of order had triumphed and the Utopian dreams of a Social Republic and all the optimism of February and March had vanished in the horrors of civil war. But the memories of the bitter fight put up by the "Army of Despair" long remained to keep alive the distrust of the bourgeoisie in many a Parisian worker's household.

Henceforward there is much to be said for the view of Lamartine and Lamennais that, although the Republic still continued for more than four years, it was really only a Republic in name. After the June Days it was experienced Orleanists or Legitimists like Thiers, Falloux, Montalembert, Odilon Barrot, and Berryer, who carried most weight in the Assembly; and, when the Assembly had completed its work of endowing the country with a Republican constitution, the nation was to elect as President a man who would work patiently to give this strange accidental republic the coup de grace.

In November, after six months of labour and much debating, the new Constitution was ready. It reflected both the retreat from the social aspirations of February and the reaction against English parliamentarism, as it had been imitated by the Charters of 1814 and 1830. The Republic now no longer guaranteed the right to work, but only undertook more cautiously to guarantee "the existence of citizens in distress, either by procuring them work within the limits of its resources or by giving relief to those who were not able to work." In its political arrangements the Constitution laid down that separation of powers was the first condition of a free Government and provided that the legislature should consist of a single chamber or Legislative Assembly. Thus the constitution-makers harked back to the traditions of the Great Revolution, but they failed to ensure that the separated parts of their new structure would work in harmony together. What, for instance, would happen if the new Legislative Assembly, to be elected by universal suffrage, should come into conflict with the new President of the Republic, who was also to be elected by universal suffrage and to enjoy very wide executive power? In vain had the moderate Republican, Jules Grévy, argued that it would be more prudent not to have a President at all. His objections had been swept aside by the eloquence of another Republican, Lamartine, who himself aspired to the Presidency and who also said that it would be an error to have the President elected by the Assembly instead of by direct universal suffrage; for an Assembly would be suspect, whereas "a nation is as incorruptible as the Ocean." Again, if there were difficulties in operating the new machinery, would it not be well to make it easy for the Constitution to be revised? But the Constituent Assembly had too much respect for its own work and held that a constitution was not a thing to be lightly tampered with. Accordingly the provisions laid down for revision were elaborate and required a vote of no less than three-quarters of the new Legislative Assembly before any changes could be made.

In December the sovereign people, Lamartine's "incorruptible nation," went once again to the polls: this time to elect the first President of the Second French Republic. Three of the Republicans who had played a prominent part in the events of the last ten months were among the candidates, Cavaignac, Lamartine and Ledru-Rollin. But these names spelt little to a nation which was by no means Republican at heart compared with another which had a meaning for the humblest peasant, a name known to all, a name covered with glory and which had gained such fresh popularity in recent years as the result of a romantic cult that it was capable of sweeping the country, almost regardless of the character and personality of its present bearer: the name of Napoleon. Already in by-elections to the Constituent Assembly in June and September a number of departments had chosen Prince Louis Napoleon, nephew of the great Emperor and, since the death of his elder brother in March 1831 and of the Duc de Reichstadt in 1832, head of the House of Bonaparte, to be their deputy. Now in December, aided by the clever and assiduous propaganda of his agents, the Prince was carried to the Presidency by an overwhelming majority. . . .

1848: THE YEAR OF GERMAN LIBERALISM

A. J. P. TAYLOR

A. J. P. Taylor, one of England's outstanding historians, successfully manages to combine the career of an Oxford don (Magdalen College) with that of a popular television personality (BBC). A prolific writer and speaker on many topics, Taylor is an expert on European diplomatic history of the nineteenth and twentieth centuries, specializing in Germany and the Austro-Hungarian monarchy. His trenchant pen has caused some critics to accuse him of prejudice against the Germans; certainly in the following excerpt from his book on German history since 1815, Taylor gives short shrift to the "liberal" and "humane" elements in the German revolutions of 1848. Yet even his harshest critics admire his writing style and admit that he bases his conclusions on sound scholarship.

1848 was the decisive year of German, and so of European, history: it recapitulated Germany's past and anticipated Germany's future. Echoes of the Holy Roman Empire merged into a prelude of the Nazi "New Order"; the doctrines of Rousseau and the doctrines of Marx, the shade of Luther and the shadow of Hitler, jostled each other in bewildering succession. Never has there been a revolution so inspired by a limitless faith in the power of ideas; never has a revolution so discredited the power of ideas in its result. The success of the revolution discredited conservative ideas; the failure of the revolution discredited liberal ideas. After it, nothing remained but the idea of Force, and this idea stood at the helm of German history from then on. For the first time since 1521, the German people stepped on to the centre of the German stage only to miss their cues once more. German history reached its turning-point and failed to turn. This was the fateful essence of 1848.

The Germany of 1848 was still, for all practical purposes, the Germany which had experienced the Napoleonic wars, still, that is to say, a predominantly rural community. Since 1815 there had been a great and continuous rise in population: from twenty-four and a half million in 1816 to thirty-four million in 1846 (or if the Austrian lands in the Confederation are included from thirty-three to forty-five million). But the proportions of town and country had remained unchanged: in Prussia 73.5 per cent of the population was classed as rural in 1816 and 72 per cent in 1846. The towns were still small, still dominated by the professional and intellectual middle classes. Industrial capitalists, still less industrial workers, did not exist as a serious political force. Even the material basis for modern industrialization had hardly been laid: in 1846 London alone consumed more coal than all Prussia raised. The revolution of 1848 was not the explosion of new forces, but the belated triumph of the *Burschenschaft,* the students of the war of liberation who were now men in their fifties. Arndt, the writer of patriotic poems against Napoleon, and even "gymnastic father" Jahn were as much the symbols of 1848 as they had been of 1813; but now their voices quavered as they sang of their youthful energy and their muscles creaked as they displayed their youthful energy in Swedish drill.

The liberals who occupied the forefront of 1848 were the men of 1813, now sobered by the long empty years. They had learnt to be cautious, to be moderate, learnt, as they thought, worldly wisdom. They had sat in the parliaments of the lesser states and had come to believe that everything could be achieved by discussion and by peaceful persuasion. Themselves dependent on the princes for their salaries or pensions as civil servants, they put belief in the good faith of princes as the first article of their policy, and genuinely supposed that they could achieve their aims by converting their rulers. Behind them were the radicals, men of unknown names and without experience: members of the same intellectual middle class, but of a younger generation — the product of the Romantic Movement, the contemporaries of Liszt, of Paganini, and of Hoffmann. These radicals were not interested in practical results. For them revolution was an end in itself, and violence the only method of politics. Yet, though they appealed constantly to force, they possessed none. The radical attempts of 1848 — Hecker's proclamation of the German republic in April and Struve's rising in September — were not even damp squibs, merely bad theatre. The radicals appealed constantly to the people, and demanded universal suffrage and a People's Republic. But they had no connection with the people of Germany, no mass support, no contact with the masses, no understanding of their needs. Thus the revolution was played out on a carefully restricted stage: on the one side the ruling princes, on the other the educated middle class in its two aspects, liberal and radical. In the end the peasant masses cleared the stage; but these peasants were disciplined conscripts in the Prussian army.

Yet the unpropertied uneducated masses were discontented and restless both in town and country; and there was in 1848 an unconscious mass revolution as well as a conscious liberal one. The inexorable increase of population made the peasants of eastern Germany land-hungry and drove the peasants of western Germany into the grip of the moneylender. The intellectual talk of revolution filtered down to the peasants, just as the intellectual ferment of the Reformation had filtered down to them in the sixteenth century. In the early months of 1848 central Europe experienced a sporadic peasant stirring, pale image of the Peasants' Revolt of 1525. In the east peasants refused their services, even attacked castles, proclaimed their freedom by appearing with clean-shaven chins; in the west they expected the community of goods and assembled in the village market places to await the general division of all property. This universal movement was altogether ignored by the middle-class liberals, and even the most extreme radicals averted their eyes. The peasants were left leaderless and unorganized. Often they turned back to their "natural leaders," the landowners. Elsewhere they accepted the directions of "authority." But everywhere the revolutionary impulse was lost. The revolution of 1848 had no agrarian programme.

The revolutionary leaders lived in the towns and therefore could not ignore so completely the movement of the urban masses. But they had no social programme, or, at best, one produced shamefacedly and *ad hoc*. The handicraft workers were being ruined by the competition of cheap mass-produced English goods; and in the winter of 1847 to 1848 the first general economic crisis devastated the larger German towns. The revolution of March 13th in Vienna and the revolution of March 18th in Berlin, which together cleared the way for the German revolution, were both glorified unemployed riots. Yet there was no connection between the political leaders and this movement of the unemployed. The town workers were given soup kitchens and relief on task work but not as part of a deliberate social policy. The liberals yielded against their economic principles in order to still the social disorder; the radicals seconded the demands of the masses not from conviction but in order to capture the masses for what they regarded as the real revolutionary aims — universal suffrage, trial by jury, election of army officers, cancelling of pensions to state officials and so on. The liberals used the mass unrest to extract concessions from the princes. The National Guard, that universal liberal expedient, for instance, was everywhere advocated as the defender of social order. The radicals, more daring, whipped up the masses in order to frighten the princes still more. But not even the few extreme radicals such as Marx, who called themselves Socialists, had any real concern for the masses or any contact with them. In their eyes the masses were the cannon fodder of the revolution; and they had no words too harsh for the masses when they wearied of filling this role. Nothing could exceed Marx's horror and disgust when his friend Engels actually took an Irish factory girl as his mistress; and Marx's attitude was symbolical of the German revolutionaries.

This divorce between the revolutionaries and the people determined the happenings of 1848. The revolution had officers but no rank and file. The old forces, on which the system of 1815 rested, succumbed to their own weakness and confusion; but no new forces took their place. There followed instead the rule of ideas, and this rule ended as soon as the old forces recovered their nerve. The German Confederation of 1815 had depended not on its own strength, but on the triangular balance of France, Austria, and Prussia. In the early months of 1848 this balance was overthrown by the revolutions in Paris, Vienna, and Berlin. The citizens of Germany — quite literally the established inhabitants of the towns — suddenly found themselves free without effort of their own. The prison walls fell, the gaolers disappeared. The Germany of intellectual conception suddenly became the Germany of established fact. For this transformation the three revolutions on the circumference were all essential. Had a single centre of power remained the German revolution would never have taken place. To consider the causes of the failure of the German revolution is thus a barren speculation. The successful revolutions were in Paris, Vienna, and Berlin. There was no successful revolution in Germany; and therefore nothing to fail. There was merely a vacuum in which the liberals postured until the vacuum was filled.

The revolution of February 24th in Paris, which overthrew Louis Philippe, evoked in all western Germany the sort of response which had been evoked by the events of the great revolution of 1789, but this time on a wider scale. In almost every state there were long-standing disputes between ruler and people — some strictly constitutional, others purely personal, most a mixture of legal grievances and private misdemeanours on the part of the prince. Typical was the conflict in Bavaria where the King had become infatuated, (to the shocked indignation of his people), with a Scotch musichall dancer who called herself Lola Montez (the same whom Swinburne immortalized as Dolores, Our Lady of Pain). Such absurdities do not cause revolutions; but they can become the critical incidents in a revolutionary situation. So, after the Paris revolution all the petty disputes which had been running on for years came to a head and were decided. In every state the existing ministers were jettisoned and more liberal ministers appointed; in every state the suffrage was extended; in some the ruler was changed, as in Bavaria where both Lola Montez and her royal admirer were driven into exile. Nowhere was there a real shifting of power; for there was no real power to shift. In 1791 and again in 1830 similar echoes of the French revolution had been stilled by the armed force of Austria and Prussia. In the early days of March 1848, Austro-Prussian interference was being again prepared; but before it could operate the power of the two military monarchies was itself shaken by the revolutions of Vienna and Berlin.

The revolution of March 13th in Vienna was a real revolution. The Metternich system was feeble without and rotten within. The administration, the finances, the army were in decay; the court was torn by disputes and faction, and the few energetic members of the Imperial family actually desired Metternich's fall. The movement of March 13th was a movement of all classes of the community. It ended old Austria for good and shattered the prestige of conservatism throughout Europe. A government of bewildered officials was hastily botched together and constantly changed under the impulse of new street demonstrations. For more than two months there was in Austria no real authority, and in Germany Austrian power vanished to nothing. Still, Austrian power had been only a secondary influence in Germany since 1815: the Austrian armies had always been centred in Italy, and Austria owed her position in Germany more to tradition and political skill than to actual strength. The really decisive event of 1848 was the revolution in Berlin; this alone made possible the brief career of German liberalism, and the ending of the Prussian revolution brought this career to a close.

Old Austria fell from deep-seated ineradicable causes which made the revolution inevitable. But the Prussian monarchy had none of the diseases which it needs a revolution to cure. Its administration was efficient, its finances in good order, the discipline of its army firm and the self-confidence of the army officers unshaken. The atmosphere of 1848 was certain to produce riots in Berlin. But according to all reasonable expectation the Prussian army was strong enough to restore order and to maintain absolutism. And so it did when the riots flared up into street fighting on March 18th. The rioters were pressed back, the streets cleared, the army was within sight of controlling all Berlin. The abnormal factor was the character of Frederick William IV. Disliking the army and hating the military traditions of his house, bewildered and depressed by the failure of his romantic ideas during the meeting of the United Diet, he could not go through with the conquest of his capital. Even on March 18th he had coupled force with exhortations. On the next day he lost his nerve altogether: promised first to withdraw the troops if the barricades were removed, and at length ordered the troops to withdraw unconditionally. By March 21st Berlin was, outwardly, in the hands of the revolution. A burgher guard patrolled the streets; the King drove through the streets wearing the revolutionary colours of national Germany; and ostensibly he embraced the revolutionary cause in the most famous of all his many phrases—"Prussia merges into Germany."

The victory of the Berlin revolution determined the course of events in Germany. Where the Prussian army had failed no prince could hope to succeed. The way was open for the liberal middle classes to put into practice their programme of a Germany united by consent. Radicalism, even if it had possessed more driving power, seemed unnecessary. After all, no one would choose the way of the barricades if the meeting of committees could achieve the same result. But the Berlin victory was illusory—hence all the disasters of the future. The Prussian army was not defeated: it was resentful, humiliated, but still confident. The army leaders were determined somehow to win back the King and to renew the struggle broken off on March 19th. Nor was Frederick William IV a convert to the liberal cause. His nerve had failed. He complained to Bismarck that he had been unable to sleep for worry. Bismarck replied roughly: "A king must be able to sleep." Short of going out of his mind (which did not happen until 1858) Frederick William would have a good night sooner or later; and thereupon Prussian policy would begin to recover its strength. Moreover Frederick William at his most distraught had all the cunning of the mentally unstable. Forced to agree to the meeting of a Prussian parliament, he tried to turn his surrender to advantage by suggesting that all Germany should send representatives to the Prussian parliament and so achieve German unification *ipso facto*. His readiness to sink Prussia in Germany was fraudulent, and the Germans were asked to entrust themselves to Frederick William's erratic impulses.

Frederick William's sham conversion was not without effect. It obscured at the decisive moment the essential ineradicable conflict between middle-class idealistic Germany and landowning conservative Prussia. If the Prussian army had emerged from the March struggles victorious, as it deserved to do, it might have gone on to conquer all Germany for the cause of order; but this development might well have provoked in Germany a real revolutionary effort and, in any case, would have estranged Prussia from national Germany for ever. As it was, Prussia slipped, almost unperceived, on to the liberal side; and when in the following year the liberal cause began to fail, the memory of the March days enabled the liberal leaders to delude themselves into taking Frederick William as their protector. In March 1848 Frederick William seemed to capitulate to the revolution; in the sequel the revolution capitulated to Frederick William in April 1849. At the time Frederick William's capitulation came a week too late. With the fall of Metternich on March 13th German liberalism felt able to do without a protector; and the military resistance in Berlin made Prussia appear, as was in fact the case, less liberal than Austria. No part of Germany responded to Frederick William's invitation. Indeed the German liberals opposed the meeting of a Prussian parliament at all. They would have preferred to limit Prussia to the separate provincial Diets, so as to prevent any rival to the German national parliament. The judgments of the German liberals were the judgments of lawyers. They recognized that the existence of Prussia was a menace to German unity; but they saw that existence incorporated in the Prussian constitution, not in the Prussian army. They supposed that Prussian militarism had been beaten for good and all, beaten so decisively that they could actually assist Frederick William without risk against his own parliament. Consistent in their legalistic outlook

they had to pretend that the surrender of Frederick William on March 19th had been voluntary; had they once admitted that the barricades and bloodshed of Berlin had played a part in the birth of the German revolution their political philosophy would have been destroyed — much as the advocates of the League of Nations had to conceal the reality that its basis was the defeat of Germany in war.

Thus the revolutions of Vienna and Berlin allowed the Germans to determine their own destinies for the first time in their history. The expression of this freedom was the National Assembly at Frankfort, concentration of the spirit of 1848. Its origin was symbolic. Not a seizure of power by revolutionaries, not a dictation of new principles from below, but a co-operation between intellectuals, self-appointed spokesmen of Germany, and the Federal Diet, still posturing as the mouthpiece of the princes, brought it into being. The learned world was, characteristically enough, caught unawares by the revolutionary situation. Fifty-one learned men were gathered at Heidelberg reading papers to each other, as learned men do, when the March storm broke. Suddenly and to their surprise their claims came true: they had to speak for Germany. They spoke with all the responsible solemnity peculiar to academic politicians, and conformed to the spirit of a non-existing constitution. Dissolving themselves as the fifty-one, they re-created themselves and their learned friends as the pre-parliament, academic ideal of a parliament by invitation. This strange nominated body conducted itself on the best parliamentary principles: held debates, passed resolutions, finally even made laws. It summoned a German Constituent Assembly, laid down the rules by which this should be elected, and then dispersed leaving a committee of fifty as the provisional government of Germany. Meanwhile the Federal Diet, abandoned by the protecting great powers, was trying to maintain its legal rights if only by giving them away. It invited the states to send new, and more liberal, representatives — the seventeen — and these seventeen also devised a plan for a National Assembly, which was then amalgamated with the plan of the pre-parliament. Thus the National Assembly which met on May 18th began its career with a background of respectability and legality.

The elections for the National Assembly were variously conducted. In those states which already possessed constitutions it was elected on the existing suffrage; in the states without constitutions, which included both Prussia and Austria, by universal suffrage. But these variations did not matter. In the limited constitutional states of western Germany, still more in unconstitutional Austria and Prussia, only the wealthy and the educated, the lawyers and the civil servants, were known; and only the known can attract votes. The result therefore was an assembly of "notables," as strictly confined to the upper middle class as if the voters had been the *pays légal* of the July monarchy. There was not a single workingman and only one peasant (a Pole from Silesia). Fifteen, mainly postmasters and customs officers (a way of getting known), ranked as lower middle class. All the rest were the well-to-do products of university education: 49 university professors; 57 highschool teachers; 157 magistrates; 66 lawyers; 20 mayors; 118 higher civil servants; 18 doctors; 43 writers; 16 Protestant pastors, 1 German Catholic and 16 Roman Catholic priests. One hundred and sixteen admitted to no profession, and among these were the few nobles; but even of the 116 far more were wealthy bourgeoisie — a few industrialists, rather more bankers and merchants. There were only sixteen army officers, and these from the liberal western states. Germany of the idea had taken on corporate life.

None of the members had experience of national politics (except a few who had sat in the Federal Diet); but most had been members of their state Chambers and all knew the technicalities of political procedure. Indeed Frankfort suffered from too much experience rather than too little: too much calculation, too much foresight, too many elaborate combinations, too much statesmanship. Hardly a vote was taken for its own sake, always for the sake of some remote consequence. The members of the Assembly wanted to give Germany a constitution; but they also wanted to show that a liberal German government could defend social order at home and the interests of Germany abroad. Almost their first act was to create a Central German Power to exercise authority in its name. But a real shifting of power was beyond their imagination, and their utmost ambition was to convert the princes to liberalism, not to overthrow them. Therefore the Central Power had to be entrusted to a prince, though a prince of reliable liberal character; and he was found in the Austrian Archduke John, brother of the late Emperor and with genuine liberal sympathies. But the choice was hardly determined by his personal qualifications: it sprang mainly from the calculation that in June 1848, Austria was more submerged by the revolution than was Prussia and would therefore be more obedient to the directions of Frankfort. Still, there was a deeper element — a survival of the traditional idea of the headship of the house of Habsburg and a belief that only under the Habsburgs could an all-embracing Germany be achieved. In June 1848, no one proposed the King of Prussia as head of Germany. To do so would have been a confession of weakness, a willingness to accept something less than complete unification. Prussia, it was assumed, would accept the overlordship of a Habsburg; but no one could suppose that the Habsburgs, even in defeat, would subordinate themselves to the King of Prussia.

The election of Archduke John was thus an expression both of the romantic Right and the radical Left; it revived the traditions of the Holy Roman Empire and at the same time asserted the democratic idea of Greater Germany. In June 1848 the confidence of German nationalism was still unbounded, and there seemed no limits, historical or geographic, to what it could achieve. John came to Frankfort, established himself as Administrator of the Reich, appointed a full set of ministers. The Federal Diet abdicated into his hands. In fact the Central Power had all the qualities of a government except power. The Minister of Foreign Affairs was not recognized by any foreign state except revolutionary Hungary — which was recognized by nobody else; the Minister of War had no soldiers; the Minister of the Interior had no means of ensuring that the orders which he issued to the governments of the German states would be obeyed. The salaries of the ministers and of Archduke John were paid out of the funds collected in 1840 for federal defence, which had remained on deposit with the Rothschilds. No national taxes were levied. The only takings of the Central Power were the voluntary subscriptions raised throughout Germany for the creation of a German fleet; and the Minister of the Navy was unique in actually having money to spend. The German Navy — a couple of discarded ships bought as a job lot in Hamburg — was the most absurd and yet the most complete expression of the spirit of 1848, of the idea of achieving power by persuasion. Unable to contemplate the real task of challenging the armed forces of Austria and Prussia, the German liberals found a substitute for the struggle for power in buying a navy by street corner collections; and the two decaying ships at their Hamburg moorings alone obeyed the Central Power of the German nation.

The essence of Frankfort was the idea of unity by persuasion. The Central Power had to show, by example, that it was fit to govern Germany and to be Germany in the eyes of foreign powers. Like a manager on trial, the Central Power produced samples of its governing capacity and, by means of orders to the princes, conducted a campaign against the unrest and disturbances in Germany. These orders the princes, gratifyingly enough, obeyed. But in achieving this success the Frankfort liberals were sawing off the branch on which they sat: only the menace of new outbreaks kept the princes obedient to Frankfort, yet Frankfort was doing its best to bring these outbreaks to an end. The members of the Assembly could not but look forward with apprehension to the time when the princes felt secure once more and they devised a highly liberal solution: the princes were to retain their armies (of which only a real revolution would deprive them), but the soldiers were to take an oath of loyalty to the German constitution. Thus the liberals confessed by implication that they could not rely on the word of the princes — the only guarantee of Frankfort's position — but their alternative was to trust the word of illiterate peasants. The device of the constitutional oath was not a success. The soldiers of the lesser states took the oath and later disregarded it; Frederick William refused to allow it to be given to the Prussian army, and the Assembly, itself meeting under the protection of Prussian soldiers, averted its eyes. The Frankfort liberals were not actuated, as is sometimes supposed, by class interest. They were not capitalists or property owners; they were lawyers and professors. Disorder and revolution offended their principles and threatened their high ideal of creating a united Germany by consent. Nothing good, they believed, could come of the intrusion of the masses into politics; and they regarded the repressive activities of the armed forces as essential to the security of the liberal cause.

The refusal of Frankfort to go with the masses, the failure to offer a social programme, was a decisive element in the failure of the German liberals. This refusal and this failure are the theme of *Germany: Revolution and Counter-Revolution,* the pamphlet which Engels wrote for Marx and which is still the best analysis of the events of 1848. But there was another, and even more important cause of failure, a disastrous mistake which Marx, Engels, and most German radicals shared. The National Assembly had come into being when the armed power of Austria and Prussia collapsed; and its prestige waned as Austrian and Prussian armed power revived. These armies won new confidence, no doubt, in the repression of internal disorder. But the prime purpose of armies is foreign war, and it was in foreign war of a sort that Austrian and Prussian absolutism were reborn. Not the social conflict, but the conflict on the national frontiers — in Bohemia, in Poland, and in Slesvig and Holstein — determined the fate of German liberalism. In the struggle against the Czechs, against the Poles, against the Danes, the German liberals unhesitatingly supported the cause of the Prussian and Austrian armies and were then surprised when these weapons were turned against themselves. Liberalism was sacrificed to the national cause.

The conflict with Czech nationalism in Bohemia had been entirely unexpected. The well-meaning German professors had assumed that Bohemia, with its educated German minority, was part of national Germany: after all, they did not count the German peasants as members of the national community, so that still less did they count peasants of any other race. The committee of fifty actually invited Palacky, intellectual pioneer of the Czech rebirth, to swell their number; and the German liberals were shocked and astonished at his famous reply of April 11th, in which he declared himself a Czech and put forward the Austrian Empire as the protector of the Slavs against either Tsarist or German rule. Palacky's letter was the most fateful document in the history of modern Germany. It asked the Germans to renounce the vast expanse of eastern Europe where they had long held cultural and economic supremacy and to accept as national Germany only those territories where the majority of the population was genuinely German. This demand was ridiculed by Germans of all shades of national opinion. To accept the national frontier would actually imply accepting something less than the frontier of the despised German Confederation; and the possession of Bohemia made all the difference between being a great and the greatest European Power. Without Bohemia Germany had but a tenuous link with the valley of the Danube and south-eastern Europe, especially before the coming of the railways; and moreover Bohemia was already one of the outstanding industrial areas of central Europe, all the more outstanding in that the industrial development of the Ruhr and Rhineland had hardly begun. But the German attitude was not determined solely by these selfish material considerations. The German nationalists of 1848 were inspired by a belief, none the less genuine for appearing to French or English judgment absurd, in the superiority of German civilization. They thought of themselves as missionaries of a great cultural cause and regarded any withdrawal in eastern Europe as a betrayal of the values of civilization. The most clear-sighted radicals, Marx and Engels above all, held rightly that industrialization and the growth of towns were the essential preliminary to political freedom, and they identified industrialization, as it had been identified historically, with German influence. In the programme of Palacky, still more in the Slav Congress which he organized at Prague in answer to the Frankfort Assembly, the German liberals and radicals saw only a movement of peasants, attempting to preserve a reactionary feudal order.

The Czech claim to Bohemia threatened all the highest ambitions of German nationalism. Without Bohemia, Germany might be a respectable national state, but neither a new Empire of Charlemagne nor the Greater Germany of radical idealism. The Slav Congress, ineffective and tentative as it was, went still further: by asserting, however feebly, the rights of Slav peasants against German traders and artisans, it challenged German hegemony throughout eastern Europe. The Frankfort Assembly inevitably supported the "national" cause. But it had no weapons of defence. As always it had to proceed by political devices and to bless the weapons of others. The only material weapon in Bohemia was the Habsburg army; and within three months of the Habsburg defeat in Vienna, to which the Frankfort Assembly owed its existence, the liberals of Frankfort were calling for a Habsburg victory in Prague. They got their way. The Imperial court, dominated by fear of the Vienna revolution, at first welcomed and encouraged the Czech movement, but this soon became too democratic for their liking. On June 12th a few Czech radicals tried to seize power in Prague, apparently with the idea of proclaiming a Bohemian republic; and this gave Windischgrätz, the Austrian general, the opportunity to subdue Prague by military force — the first victory of the counter-revolution in central Europe. This was a victory for Habsburg militarism and therefore a step towards the defeat of German nationalism. Yet the German liberals, blinded by hatred and fear of the Czechs, put themselves on the Habsburg side and welcomed the victory of Windischgrätz as if it had been their own. They had always recognized the national claims of the Magyars, a people with a continuous history and a flourishing culture; and they believed that the victory of Windischgrätz had established the German character of the non-Hungarian provinces of the Austrian Empire. The German and Magyar nationalists both assumed that the Habsburg lands would be henceforward held together only by a personal link, and that Magyar-dominated Hungary and the Greater Germany into which the rest of the Austrian Empire would be incorporated would be united in a common anti-Slav policy. The German liberals were confident that the Habsburg power was, as it were, "captured" for German nationalism, so confident that, instead of resisting the meeting of a central Austrian parliament at Vienna as the expression of the unity of the Habsburg lands, they welcomed and aided it, believing — quite wrongly — that it would be a further instrument for their national and liberal ends.

Events in Bohemia brought the Germans on to the side of the Habsburgs. Still they could plead that the Habsburg Empire now had a liberal parliament. Events in Prussian Poland, however, not merely brought the German liberals on to the side of the Hohenzollerns, but even led them to support the King of Prussia against the Prussian parliament. The Polish situation differed fundamentally from the Czech, in that the Poles were a historic nation whose existence could be neither disputed nor ignored. Polish liberty was an essential element in the radical creed. The extreme radicals believed that they could achieve their programme only by means of a revolutionary war; and they proposed to provoke a war with Russian Tsardom by fulfilling in the Grand Duchy of Posen the promises of constitutional freedom made both for Posen and the Russian Kingdom of Poland in the Treaty of Vienna. By a stroke of amateur Machiavellianism the German radicals who had denounced the "Vienna system" for thirty years were now designing to conduct a war against Russia in its name. War with Russia, not love for the Poles, was the motive of their policy; they intended to renew German claims in Poland, once Russia was defeated. West Prussia was mainly inhabited by Poles, yet was excluded from the promises of 1815, since it had not been torn from the Kingdom of Prussia by Napoleon and so did not need to be restored by the Treaty of Vienna; as a result the radicals did not trouble themselves with the claims of the West Prussian Poles. On the other hand, the Grand Duchy of Posen, though indisputably part of the old Kingdom of Poland, had a considerable German minority; so that the radicals were proposing to establish Polish national rights in districts sometimes with but few Polish inhabitants.

In the first distracted days after the March rising the weak Prussian Government of well-meaning liberals was swept along by the radical current and admitted in the Grand Duchy the autonomy promised in 1815. The Prussian army was withdrawn to barracks, a Polish force was brought into being, and the administration was put into the hands of the Poles. This produced a conflict of a character quite unexpected by the radical strategists. Tsar Nicholas I, wiser than the counter-revolutionaries of 1792, accepted the opinion of his Chancellor, Nesselrode, that the German revolution would disintegrate if left to itself, and decided against intervention. The Germans in Posen, refusing to be the victims of a political manoeuvre, resisted the Polish authorities and appealed to their fellow-Germans for support. This was the opportunity for the Prussian army chiefs. At the end of April the Prussian general in Posen disregarded the civil government, defeated the Polish forces, and expelled the Polish administrators. The Grand Duchy was to be split up: the larger part was declared to be German, and even in the fragment left to the Poles the Germans were to be especially privileged. No element of national equality remained. The radicals of Berlin, baulked of their war with Tsardom, and the Poles of Posen, denied their freedom, appealed to the National Assembly at Frankfort to act on its pro-Polish phrases and to compel the Prussian Government to keep its word.

It was an awkward demand for the Frankfort liberals. They wished to appear all-powerful in Germany, yet knew that they were impotent to compel the Prussian Government or any other. They wished to defend German rights; yet they dared not do so on the basis of nationality statistics (which justified some of the German claims), for these statistics would justify the claims of the Czechs in Bohemia. William Jordan, one of the most respected liberal leaders, solved the dilemma: the right of the stronger, he said, must decide, and "healthy national egoism" demanded that the Grand Duchy of Posen should become German. In these phrases, welcomed by the liberal majority, the Frankfort liberals delivered themselves to the Prussian army and, by an inevitable logic, delivered German liberalism first to Bismarck and later to Hitler. The right of the stronger which they evoked would then be turned against them, and "healthy national egoism" would be translated into "blood and iron." On July 27th the Frankfort Assembly rejected the radical complaints and bestowed its blessing on the Prussian army in Posen as it had already blessed the Austrian army in Bohemia.

There was a strange result. The Prussian parliament had been elected on the same day and with the same franchise as the National Assembly, but it was very differently composed. The wealthy, respectable candidate went to Frankfort; the poorer, more impatient candidate made the shorter journey to Berlin. The Prussian parliament was dominated by radicals from East Prussia, who had learnt political reality in bitter struggles with the neighbouring Junkers. These radicals cared no more for Polish rights than did the Frankfort liberals, but they were eager to force a breach between the Junkers and the Tsar, the Junkers' protector. In September the Prussian parliament rejected the partition of the Grand Duchy of Posen, and, a month later, demanded the execution of the promises of 1815. The Prussian radicals, hostile to the Tsar and jealous of Frankfort, dreamt even of transforming the Prussian state into a Polish-German federation, aloof from national Germany. The estrangement between Frankfort and Berlin was complete. The Prussian parliament was offensive in itself to German nationalism, for it implied the existence of a Prussia distinct from Germany; but it became doubly offensive when it renounced the claims of "healthy national egoism" in Posen. The Frankfort liberals, who had applauded the victory of the Prussian army in Posen, were thus led on to desire a victory of the Prussian army in Berlin — despite the fact that the defeat of the Prussian army in Berlin had been the essential preliminary to the Frankfort parliament.

In the autumn of 1848 there were yet more immediate reasons for Frankfort's dependence on the Prussian army. The third and most deeply felt frontier issue of 1848 was the question of Slesvig and Holstein, two duchies which had long been under the sovereignty of the King of Denmark; Holstein inhabited entirely by Germans and a member of the German

Confederation, Slesvig inhabited partly by Germans, partly by Danes, and outside the Confederation. The legal tangle — the relation of the Duchies with each other, with the German Confederation, with the King of Denmark, with Denmark, their position in the treaty structure of Europe, their laws of succession provided endless material for controversy and confusion; but the essential question was clear. Did the principle of German national unity override treaty rights and international law? The number of Germans involved was not great, half a million at most — the theoretical challenge all the more marked. The problem of the two Duchies was the breaking-point of the traditional idea of personal sovereignty, for neither the Danes nor the Germans were prepared to leave the Duchies in their former position. In 1848 Denmark too had its constitutional revolution; and the Danish liberals were determined to incorporate Slesvig in the Danish constitutional state. Once Denmark abandoned personal union, there was something to be said for the German case, much more than for the German case in Bohemia or in Poland. All the more unexpected to the German liberals was the reaction of foreign opinion. These liberals were educated men of high culture, who attached great importance to the judgment of liberals in the western countries. Hitherto they had won foreign approval. German nationalists of all shades of opinion had recognized the claims of Hungary; foreign observers knew nothing of the Czech case in Bohemia and unanimously accepted the German version of a reactionary conspiracy; and the Frankfort hostility to Polish claims was altogether dwarfed by the Tsarist repression in Russian Poland. But in the question of Slesvig and Holstein foreign liberals saw only the bullying of a small nation by a great one; English, French, Italian liberals united to condemn Germany. The German liberals were not shaken by this condemnation. They were too convinced of the rightness of their cause. Rather they concluded that there was a deliberate conspiracy against Germany;

if western liberalism condemned German nationalism in Slesvig and Holstein, so much the worse for western liberalism. In fact, the question of Slesvig and Holstein made the first, not very marked, but yet decisive breach between the German nationalist movement and the liberals of western Europe, a breach in which the western liberals, ironically enough, were on the side of the "Vienna settlement."

The dispute between Denmark and the Duchies broke into open conflict as early as March 1848; and the pre-parliament had already set on foot a federal war against the Danes. But when it came to the point national Germany, so sensitive in its honour, so vast in its claims, had no forces with which to conduct a war even against Denmark. The only agent of national Germany was the Prussian army; the liberal ministry in Prussia responded to the appeal from Frankfort, and the Prussian generals, still humiliated by the March days, obeyed the orders of the civilian ministers. During the early summer the Prussian army made easy headway against the Danes. But it soon became clear that Prussia would have to face more formidable opponents. Both England and Russia were resolved to uphold the settlement of 1815 and to keep the control of the entrance to the Baltic securely in harmless Danish hands. A European war threatened. Enthusiastic liberals from south Germany clamoured for "sanctions" — federal execution was the current term — against Denmark, whatever the risk; but the risk would have to be borne by conservative Prussian officers. Prussia was faced with a war from which she could not possibly gain: she would probably be defeated, but even if she won, the advantage would go to the German liberals, who would thus be all the stronger to destroy Prussia's independence. Therefore at the end of August Prussia concluded an armistice with Denmark and left the national cause to fend for itself.

Prussia had thus openly defied the authority of the National Assembly and the Central Power. The German liberals were at last inescapably faced with the problem of power. Powerless to coerce Denmark, they yet had to coerce Prussia into renewing the war against Denmark or else to confess the impotence of the national idea on the strength of which they had based their political philosophy. The ministers of the Central Power realized that their orders carried no weight with the Prussian army; but a motley majority of the Assembly — national idealists, radical extremists, pro-Austrians eager to humiliate Prussia — broke away from their leadership and refused to acknowledge the armistice. The ministry resigned. But no new ministry, ready to take on an open conflict with Prussia, could be formed. The coalition of idealists and impossibilists dissolved. The Assembly was compelled to eat its own words and to approve the armistice which a week before it had rejected. A ministry openly favourable to the two Great Powers came into existence. This betrayal of the German cause was too much for the radicals who had been growing increasingly impatient with the moderation and statesmanship of the liberal majority. There were radical riots in many western German towns and, finally, on September 26th, in Frankfort itself. The National Assembly, with no forces of its own, had to appeal to the King of Prussia, whom only a fortnight before it had solemnly condemned. Prussian troops restored order; and from the end of September the National Assembly and Central Power met under the protection of Prussian bayonets. In March 1848 national Germany had condescendingly tolerated the Prussian state. In October the Prussian state allowed national Germany to prolong its existence.

National Germany owed its temporary success to the defeat of the two military monarchies in March; yet, in order to defend the "national" cause in Bohemia and in Posen, it had welcomed the reassertion of Austrian and Prussian military power. In the autumn of 1848 the reviving monarchies took up the struggle with their own capitals; but so far as national opinion was concerned with opposite results. Habsburg victory over the October revolution in Vienna made Austria unpopular, Hohenzollern victory over the abortive November revolution in Berlin made Prussia popular in Germany. The conflict in Vienna was a conflict over the character of the Austrian Empire. Was it, as the Germans of Frankfort and Vienna and the Magyars alike held, a union of two states, one German, the other Magyar? Or was it, as the Habsburg ministers, the Austrian aristocracy, and the Czechs and Croats alike held, a single Empire in which no single nationality held a preponderant or privileged position? The Habsburg Court had recovered from the utter confusion and hopelessness of the spring. There was now an effective ministry, its outstanding personality, Bach, a pre-March radical, won over to the cause of a centralized and reformed Austrian Empire. This ministry, supported by a majority of the Austrian parliament — a majority partly non-German, but also composed of Germans who subordinated their nationality to the maintenance of the Empire — was determined to undo the concessions made to Hungary in the days of collapse and to reduce Hungary from an independent state to a province of the Empire. The success of their plan would be as much a defeat for German as for Hungarian nationalism; for no one imagined that national Hungary could be incorporated in the German national state, and the entire Austrian Empire would therefore stand aloof from Germany. Early in October the radicals of Vienna tried to prevent the sending of troops to Hungary; and on October 6th Vienna broke into revolution.

The October revolution was a revolution in favour of an independent Hungary and a national Germany; but neither came to its assistance. Hungary had an organized and equipped army, but failed to use it, partly from constitutional scruples against crossing the Austrian frontier, more from a reluctance to make sacrifices in what seemed to the Hungarians a foreign cause. National Germany had no forces and therefore fell back on the most disastrous of idealist weapons — it displayed moral sympathy. On October 27th, while the civil war in Austria was still being fought, the Frankfort Assembly resolved that, where German and non-German lands were under the same ruler, they should be united only by a personal tie. Thus the Assembly committed itself to the programme of the partition of the Austrian Empire at the very moment when that programme was being shot to pieces on the Vienna barricades. Early in November the Austrian army conquered Vienna and so ended all hope of a Greater Germany. The imbecile Emperor Ferdinand was replaced by his young energetic nephew Francis Joseph; a new ministry was formed under Felix Schwarzenberg, ruthless, cynical advocate of the policy of military power. The first act of the new ministry was to execute Robert Blum, a radical member of the Frankfort Assembly who had fought on the side of the Vienna revolution; its second to denounce the Frankfort resolution in favour of the partition of Austria. The Austrian parliament, now purged of its German radicals, was left temporarily in being, occupying itself in futile constitution-making until its dissolution in the following March. But in liberal German eyes Austria reverted to despotism in November 1848, and to a despotism flagrantly anti-German. The dreamers and radicals still hoped for a miracle which would restore Austria to liberalism and to Germany; the moderates and realists abandoned Austria and consoled themselves by pretending that the inclusion of Austria in Germany had never been part of their national programme.

In Prussia too, militarism was victorious in the autumn of 1848, but victorious without violence and without a breach with Frankfort. Here the struggle between King and Parliament was not national, but strictly constitutional. The Prussian parliament wished to enforce an oath of constitutional loyalty on the Prussian army. This demand did not interest Frankfort, which — having failed with its own constitutional oath —

was jealous that the Berlin parliament should not succeed. In fact, many Frankfort liberals, regarding the Berlin parliament as a rival and more radical body, desired its defeat. Having backed the loser in Austria, they were the more eager to be on the winning side in Prussia and, by offering the king their moral support (threadbare as this was), to create the impression that they had contributed to his success. As one of the liberal leaders said: "It is in the interests of the National Assembly that the Prussian Crown should be victorious over its parliament, but that it should achieve this victory with the help of the National Assembly." Frederick William and his generals did not need this help, though Frankfort tried to claim credit for offering it. In November, Frederick William appointed an openly reactionary ministry and broke with his parliament. It was first moved to a provincial town, and then dissolved; and the king issued a restricted constitution by decree. The parliamentary radicals attempted to resist. They refused to leave Berlin, held meetings of parliament in various halls and finally in cafés and beer cellars, they appealed to the inhabitants of Prussia to refuse to pay taxes. Nothing happened: taxes were paid, the radical deputies were chased home. There had been no real victory of the revolution in Berlin in March; therefore no real counter-revolution was necessary in November. The Prussian army and the Prussian governing class moved back into positions from which the king's erratic feebleness, not the strength of the revolution, had ejected them.

By the end of 1848 the power of the two German powers was restored, the Central Power therefore became utterly meaningless. The Frankfort Assembly still debated. The idealists who had hoped to disregard both Great Powers and to build Germany on ideas were discredited. It was the turn of the moderate men — professors determined as professors so often are to demonstrate that they were men of the world, politicians from the petty states who wished to show their practical wisdom. The two German powers existed; therefore Germany should hitch herself to one of them, should, by her superior political cunning, "capture" one of them for the German cause. It was futile to try to capture Austria: her November victory had been too emphatic, her anti-national policy too blatant. But it was possible to interpret the defeat of the Prussian parliament as a defeat for particularism, possible to believe that Frederick William still held to his romantic vision of a Prussia merged into Germany. Thus there came into being the party of Little Germany, the sensible men who would be content with something less than complete unification. Greater Germany was a creed, a conviction; Little Germany an expedient, a temporizing with reality. No national principle could underlie the programme of giving only some Germans national unity; and in fact all Little Germans were Greater Germans at heart — only they were prepared to postpone the realization of the full programme. No one at Frankfort ever argued that Little Germany was better than Greater Germany. The Little Germans argued that Little Germany could be secured now and that it could be secured peacefully, without revolution. They were opposed by the idealists who would accept nothing less than the whole; by the radicals who were Greater Germans simply because this needed a revolution; by the Roman Catholics who feared Prussian rule; and by the friends and dependants of Austria. The Little German liberals devised a moderate monarchist constitution with limited suffrage and the King of Prussia as Emperor; but they could not carry this against the coalition of democrats, clericals, and pro-Austrians. To win over the democratic vote, they jettisoned all their liberal restrictions and moderation except the one item of the Emperor. An astonishing compromise resulted. On the one hand the Frankfort Assembly excluded Austria from Germany and offered the Imperial Crown to Frederick William IV — the Little German programme. On the other hand it established in this Little Germany a centralized democratic constitution based on uni-versal suffrage, which was only compatible with the victory of Greater German ideas. Thus even at the moment of its abject failure the Frankfort Assembly postulated the ultimate destiny of Germany and of Prussia: Prussia could dominate Germany, but only on condition of serving the national German cause.

In April 1849, a deputation went from Frankfort to offer the Imperial Crown to Frederick William IV. The offer had been expected in Berlin, and there had been long discussions between the king and his reactionary ministers. The Prussian ministers and generals would have nothing to do with national Germany. They were ready to use the opportunity of the confusion in Germany for some land-grabbing in the old Prussian style; but apart from this they wished to renew the conservative partnership with Austria. Frederick William, on the other hand, could not altogether resist the romantic prospect of the Imperial Crown if only it could be freed from its democratic associations. He would have liked to accept the Crown on condition that it was offered to him by the princes. Urgent and desperate promptings from his advisers only induced him to give this acceptance a negative form: he would not "pick up a Crown from the gutter," would not accept the Crown unless it was offered to him by the princes. This answer he gave to the Frankfort deputation on April 3rd. They heard only the refusal, for they knew by now that the princes would not voluntarily surrender their sovereignty. Prussia would not, Frankfort could not, force the princes into unity. The liberal revolution had reached its term.

With the failure of the mission to Berlin the history of the Frankfort Assembly was over. The moderate men, the men who shrank from violence, went home. Only the radical minority remained. Late in the day, with the revolutionary flood ebbing away to nothing, they tried to put into practice the revolutionary programme and to evoke a real revolution in Germany. They proclaimed that the German constitution had come into force, called for radical revolutions in the German state, and decreed the elections for the German parliament for July 15th. The elections never took place. Rhetoric could not change the practical fact that the only force in Germany was the Prussian army; and this army easily subdued the radical risings in Dresden, the Bavarian Palatinate, and Baden, which the Frankfort appeal had provoked. The Assembly, or rather its radical rump, was chased by the Prussian army from Frankfort to Stuttgart in Wurtemberg, and from Stuttgart it was chased out of existence. Sole remnant of national Germany was the Archduke John, still clinging to a theoretical Central Power in order to prevent a Prussian domination of Germany. In December he surrendered his title into the joint hands of Austria and Prussia. The German revolution was defeated, and liberal Germany never to be renewed.

As is usual after failure, every man drew the conclusion that the movement would have succeeded if his advice had been followed, and most despaired of the stupidity of their fellows. A few extreme radicals remained faithful to the revolutionary cause and hoped for a more violent revolution in the future. Next time, they believed, the masses must be drawn in; the cause of national union must be adorned with the attractions of Socialism. This was the programme of Marx and Engels to which they devoted the rest of their life, until their national starting-point was almost forgotten. They advocated Socialism so as to cause a revolution; only much later did their followers suppose that they had advocated revolution in order to accomplish Socialism. The radicals who did not despair of Germany were few. Far more accomplished their own revolution by emigrating to the freedom of the United States. German emigration had already begun on a big scale, more than a hundred thousand a year, in the early 'forties. It dwindled to fifty thousand in 1848, when it seemed that Germany might be at last a place worth living in. After 1848 it soared once more,

running at a steady average of more than a quarter of a million a year throughout the eighteen-fifties. These emigrants were the best of their race — the adventurous, the independent, the men who might have made Germany a free and civilized country. They brought to the United States a contribution of inestimable value, but they were lost to Germany. They, the best Germans, showed their opinion of Germany by leaving it for ever.

Like the radical emigrants, most liberals too were disillusioned by their experience of practical politics. Many withdrew to academic studies or served Germany by applying science to practical needs. Some turned from politics to industry and finance. So Hansemann, most liberal of the Prussian ministers of 1848, founded the Discontogesellschaft, one of the greatest of German banks. The liberal politicians who remained politicians resolved to be more moderate and practical than ever. Their faith in the strength of their idea was destroyed; therefore they believed that liberal Germany must be achieved by subtlety and guile. But it would be wrong to suppose that the liberals of Germany vanished or that liberal convictions counted for nothing in Germany after 1848. The professors, the lawyers, the civil servants of the lesser states, remained predominantly liberal: they were still liberal in 1890 and even, for the most part, in 1930. But in 1848 they were a serious and respected political force. After 1848 they counted for less and less and, at last, for nothing at all.

The real significance of the revolution of 1848 was not so much its failure at the time, but the effect of its failure in the future. After 1850 there began in Germany a period of industrial development, after 1871 an industrial revolution. Economic power passed within a generation into the hands of industrial capitalists. Industrial capitalists, it is commonly held, are in politics liberal; but this view is an abbreviation of the real course of events. Industrial capitalists, like all business men, judge everything by the standard of success. A good business man is one who succeeds; a bad business man is one who "fails." When industrial capitalists enter politics they apply the same standard and adopt as their own the party and outlook which prevails. In England and the United States the struggle between liberalism and arbitrary power had long been fought out. The execution of Charles I, the overthrow of the army, and the Glorious Revolution in England, the defeat of the redcoats and royal government in America, established the great principles of constitutional freedom and the rule of law. The English and American capitalists found the civilian politicians and lawyers in control. Therefore they too became liberals, advocates of individual freedom and upholders of constitutional government. In France, despite the great revolution, the verdict of success was less clear: therefore the industrial capitalists were confused — some became republicans, some Bonapartists, some corrupt and unprincipled. But in Germany there could be no doubt where success lay. The German capitalists became dependants of Prussian militarism and advocates of arbitrary power as naturally and as inevitably as English or American capitalists became liberals and advocates of constitutional authority. Where Anglo-Saxon capitalists demanded *laissez-faire*, German capitalists sought for state leadership; where Anglo-Saxon capitalists accepted democracy, however grudgingly, German capitalists grudgingly accepted dictatorship. This was the fateful legacy of 1848.

FINIS, RESULTS AND AFTER

VEIT VALENTIN

Veit Valentin was the great historian of the German liberal movement of 1848. His devotion to liberalism caused the Nazis to oust him from his academic posts and to withdraw his books from circulation, although he was neither a Socialist nor a Communist and was of pure "Aryan" descent. In 1933 Valentin took refuge in England, coming to the United States in 1939, where he lectured at various institutions and was a Rockefeller research associate at the Library of Congress. He died in Washington, D. C., in 1947, at the age of 61. The following excerpt is from the English translation and abridgment of his definitive two-volume work on the German revolutions of 1848, in which he extolled the liberal nature of the revolutionaries and praised the work of the Frankfort Parliament. Despite the immediate failure of the revolutions, Valentin claimed that the liberal spirit lived on in Germany.

THE GERMAN Revolution of 1848–49 falls into five sections: the period of preparation, the first outbreak and apparent victory, social revolutionary and nationalistic threats, consequently the beginning of the counter-revolution, second outbreak, and finally the victory of the counter-revolution.

The pre-history of the Revolution naturally stretches back to the popular movement of 1830, even back to the Napoleonic Era and the Wars of Liberation. I have confined myself to the actual "period of preparation," the 'forties, in which we already find all the elements of the democratic movement of 1848–49: the decay of Metternich's system and the movement of the classes in Austria, the Prussian constitutional question and the United Diet, the Bavarian State crisis provoked by Lola Montez, the oddities and vitality of the petty states, the insufficiency of the German Confederation, and of German National efforts at reform, the splitting-up of the classes, the unemployment and under-nourishment of the lower classes, the yeasty thinking, the urge, the unrest in intellectual and artistic creation: these all point with certainty to the eruption; feeling and inward tension, the sharpness of tone and ruthless consistency of the final demands were already entirely revolutionary.

"The first outbreak and apparent victory" embraces the period of the March–April Revolution of 1848 and the developments up to June. The democratic movement met with brilliant success everywhere; the men who had been in opposition were called to responsibility; fighting only occurred at a few points, in the end the new ideas achieved a political victory, in Berlin the authoritarian and militaristic state was unquestionably humiliated; the newly-awakened national will was to have strong executive organs created for it to express German political being in its entirety; this national feeling swamped everything, it turned against Denmark, against Poland and Russia, and in internal matters, firmly trusting in the honesty and vitality of the

From Veit Valentin, 1848: *Chapters of German History* (London, 1940), pp. 422–427, 431–433, 446–450, 454, 456–458. By permission of George Allen & Unwin Ltd.

royal power-complex and its will to reform, it collected patriotic ideas and masses together as a barrier against violently revolutionary, socialistically minded republicanism. The apparent victory ended with the assembling of the German National Assembly at Frankfort and the formation of a provisional executive. A Vicar of the Empire with responsible Imperial ministers guaranteed legal transition to a final national form of life, the formation and carrying-out of an Imperial Constitution for the new Germany. Many saw in the Imperial Vicariate the beginning of a centrally built-up Greater Germany under the Lorraine-Meran dynasty.

The "social-revolutionary and national threat, consequently the beginning of the counter-revolution" comprises the period from June to November 1848. The bearers of the revolutionary idea were deeply dissatisfied. The new era was not new at all. The advisory assemblies in all German residencies and especially in Frankfort did not touch the country's real needs. Workmen's leagues came into being, artisans' and trade congresses. The *Neue Rheinische Zeitung* raised the complaint of communism. Democratic congresses in Frankfort and Berlin sought to prepare the continuance of the Revolution. There was much resentment at the alliance of the higher and middle classes of the citizens with the old powers, and their optimism, so easily satisfied. The old March revolutionary front was exploded. March ministers were seen to be powerless and behind them was the old all-powerful phalanx of the bureaucracy, there was militia, there were popular assemblies, and behind them the old military power; people read newspapers and listened to speeches — but in the separate states the princely and aristocratic will to rule was as dominant as ever. Others besides the Germans acquired nationalistic ideas. The Poles hammered at the doors of Prussia; Slavs, Hungarians, and Italians threatened to break up the Austrian Empire. In addition to all this, the idea of a strong, all-embracing Germany went against the idea of the Prussian State, its traditions of a great power, its conditions of life, its territorial form — but just as much against that Napoleonic creation, Bavaria, and all the individual dwarf and petty states.

The new central executive and the Frankfort Parliament, needed to produce national strength and much outward success. Their failure in the matter of the Malmö armistice roused both the nationalistic and social-revolutionary elements to violent effort. The Austrian army defeated the nationalities at Cracow and Prague; the September revolts in the Rhine and Main territory forced the new authorities to make use of the old measures of force.

The Viennese October Revolution fought despairingly for a liberated Greater Germany against the fettered Greater Austria of dynasty, feudalism, clericalism, and military power. Then the Prussian monarchy also ventured to strike a blow against the constitutional National Assembly, which, in defiance of landed proprietors and regiments of guards, was endeavouring to turn Prussia into a democratic State amenable to law. Frankfort and Berlin, which should have joined forces, while Austria was weak, did not, however, come together.

"The second outbreak" covers the period from November 1848 to April 1849. Austria displayed with increasing acerbity the will to become a centralized Imperial State, the "rebels" in Italy and Hungary were suppressed, the realization of a united German Empire was frustrated, but also the so-called Little-Germany solution which continued the Gagern programme. Bavaria and all the petty states were shaken by unrest and trouble of every kind. This particularism was intimately allied with the patriotism which was striving everywhere in Germany to bring about a free and national State. The Frankfort Constitution was actually adopted by all German popular representatives except in Austria and Liechtenstein. The refusal of the King of Prussia to accept the Imperial crown at the hands of the people, and still more the refusal to accept the Constitution, even in a modified form, caused the popular movement to flame up again all over Germany. This rising had been in preparation for months. Once more there was a combination of national and social-revolutionary motives, and these contradictions doomed the whole movement to failure.

The fight for the Constitution was more than a last despairing attempt to bring the work of the Frankfort Parliament to some sort of positive conclusion. It also meant a last bold attempt to seize upon all that the March Revolution of 1848 had failed to achieve. The "Victory of the Counter-Revolution" in Germany lasted from April to July 1849. Outwardly it includes the civil war in Saxony and Baden, the movements in Bavaria, Württemberg, Thuringia, and the Rhineland. The European great power, Prussia, deliberately and consciously threw her military strength into the balance on the side of Austria and Russia. The battle against the Revolution had become a great question of foreign policy. The war with Denmark had already shown that Prussia had no conception of such policy. She repeatedly gave way to Russian pressure; English favour and French friendship could not be counted on; but much more might have been made of them, for the Western Powers delighted in the quarrel between the two Germanic powers. Prussia overpowered the patriots under the name of rebels, and thought to replace them by a lukewarm policy of "Union." The more modest goal of a North German Confederation might have been attainable if well prepared beforehand. But Prussia grasped at South Germany and the end of the revolutionary period shows a totally different picture. Prussia, hope of all progressives, had disappointed everybody, had become an executioner of the Counter-Revolution, without any gain to herself: Austria was maintaining herself with astonishing vitality against all comers and had every prospect of gaining the sympathies in South and West Germany that Prussia had thrown away.

The German Revolution was over, but its spirit was not dead. Revolution had already laid latent in the preparatory era, as Counter-Revolution in the Revolution itself; and in Counter-Revolution again the later period of reform lay latent, which was to lead to the foundation of the Empire in 1871. But this was not all; the victory of the Counter-Revolution in Germany was also a victory of the party of constitutional reform over parliamentary and social-revolutionary democrats; the communists, who had warned against half-measures, above all against trustfulness, were shown to have been in the right. The moderates sank wounded and fainting into impotence; the extremists confronted one another in bitterest enmity; dictatorial authority, with its militarist-capitalistic idea of a Great Power — and Marxism.

The victory of the Counter-Revolution in Germany bankrupted the previous revolutionary methods and ideas. Politics became materialistic, intellect, and culture too. The active revolution had been imbued with ideas. The reaction was avowedly exactly the reverse. The naïve pleonasm *Realpolitik* was born at this time. Authoritative power policy, natural-scientific over-assertion of self and Marxian socialism equalled each other in materialism. Nothing proves more saliently the actual importance of the idea in history than the embitterment with which it was opposed and the often unconscious hypocrisy with which it was used as an excuse.

Many observers of the German Revolution of 1848–49 have refused to permit the name of revolution to be applied to it. Certainly, Latin and Slavonic revolutions have exhausted the last possibility of revolutionary action; the English revolution of the seventeenth century was full of stronger tension, although it had one curious characteristic in common with the German revolution, which was, to return to a new legitimacy as rapidly as possible. Every nation makes revolution in accordance with its inner nature. War and foreign policy produce an absolute measure of the best super-national achievement: revolutions are an individual revelation of a people's soul. Revolutions that are choked down are apt to be indigestible; the Revolution of 1848–49 was not able to develop itself to the full, and the German people are still suffering for it today. The Counter-Revolution has shaped German destiny all the more energetically since. The attempt at revolution had been made, with its apparent successes. Since then, all German princes and statesmen have reckoned with revolution and taken counter-measures against it. The fissure had opened, innocence was no more. Experience raised a strident voice. One might say that it took the Counter-Revolution in Germany to demonstrate the full historical existence of the Revolution. . . .

Bruno Bauer called the Revolution of 1848–49 "the bourgeois revolution" and thus helped to found a conception which, although completely erroneous, has prevailed to this day.

The designation "bourgeois" has been commonly used for the Revolution of 1848–49 in opposition to "proletarian" or "socialistic." Certainly the urban middle-class, though in process of decay, stood in the forefront of the movement and its main objective was the reform of the Constitution. But the fate of the population was decided by auxiliary factors, working beside and behind the scenes — the agrarian revolts, the associations of artisans and workmen, the striving after new forms and conditions of social intercourse in Germany, often with a strong undercurrent of philosophic principles, a sharply critical tendency, a revolutionary inspiration. The battle for a new Constitution was in itself by no means hopeless, and would perhaps have met with success had it not been for the radical minorities whose existence rendered it easier for the forces of counter-revolution to split up and weaken the bourgeoisie. Apart from the sociological development which sought, not to consolidate, but to separate and build up anew — the intellectual spirit of the popular movement was as determinedly bourgeois in the one camp as it was deliberately revolutionary in the other. It is these contrasting and conflicting forces which make the aspect of the time so contradictory. Counter-revolutionaries pointed mockingly to many philistine and puritan elements among the new forces; but far more marked was the spirit of youthful enthusiasm which informed the movement to the last. The young were glad to be young, they were proud of their youth; they called things fearlessly by their right names and the very boldness and uncompromising spirit of their youth awakened confidence and won them followers from among the simple hearts of the lower classes who did not want to be pedantically instructed, but led with enthusiasm. Sometimes a little foolishness is both subtle and more fruitful than too much wisdom; the rising classes were all for emotion and sentiment; their strongest feature was a blind natural urge and they sought passion at which they could take fire. They believed because they wished to believe and had need of sacrifice, often the sacrifice of their very lives. It has rightly been said that revolutions bring about outbreaks of both sensual and religious emotion. Something absolute arose and masks were laid aside. Nature demanded her eternal rights. It was the task of the leaders to find an ethical and reasonable justification in opposition to everything conventional. Everything in reason was supposed to be attainable. No doubt the last great battle for the Constitution was beset by stupidities; nothing is easier than to prove this; but it is quite unimportant. The new, free, strong, just Germany was sought after with passionate heroism by the blinded, excited, newly-awakened combatants; they, too, wished for better times; why not, indeed? Every true fighter battles for himself and for his cause at the same time. The two things should not be separated. In any case it was anything but bourgeois to possess so much imagination, such a capacity for sacrifice. It was these qualities which made the conquered of 1849 into pioneers for the eternal revolution of humanity.

Naturally there were fanatics and quacks in this German revolution, as in every other. The masses were too enraptured by what was new for its own sake to distinguish the charlatan and the profiteer at first sight. This condition of things most bitterly affected the old guard of 1848; their seriousness and experienced knowledge was suddenly challenged and overwhelmed by unbalanced hysteria; disgusted, the former opposition either retired altogether from the scene or sought alliance with the older powers, being usually unable to discern the element of strength in the new, young oppositional spirit.

This procedure meant something decisive in German social history and in the later development of the German party system. Before 1848 there were many signs that a new lower-class might be formed in Germany on a broad basis, consisting of artisans, employees, servants, working-men, peasant-farmers, and small shopkeepers; a class that would have been democratic in the widest sense of the word; that is, national, parliamentary, and social, and which would not have been disinclined to acknowledge a democratic emperor. The Counter-Revolution prevented the development of this class and thus the evolution of such a party. The very name of "democratic" vanished for a time. In South Germany, it was replaced by "People's Party" (Volkspartei). The name and conception "social-democratic," which we have seen appearing in Baden, Saxony, and Electoral Hesse, was destined to a splendid career later. . . .

Comparison with all other revolutions in modern history shows the German Revolution of 1848–49 to have had the smallest percentage of deeds of violence, also of crimes against property. During his revolt, Friedrich Hecker ran along the ranks, urging his men to take nothing without paying for it on the nail, since the villagers were already lamenting as if a band of robbers were approaching. When, during the Berlin March Revolution, certain people threatened to take a fancy to the silver vessels in the Jerusalemer Church, Wolff the sculptor, who had marched to revolution in his dressing-gown, girt with a sabre and crowned with a flapping broad-brimmed hat, pretended to be seized with revolutionary fury, bore the vessels off and secreted them in his house until things quieted down. There was no organized revolutionary terror; a couple of isolated acts such as the tearing down of the Dresden opera house were mere individual excesses. But there is much evidence that the soldiers beat their prisoners, and the treatment of political prisoners in convict prisons was often purposely harsh.

The German Revolution of 1848 erected no guillotines and held no extraordinary courts of a purely political nature. No one except Prince Metternich was banished; there was no confiscation of fortunes, no holding-up of salaries, no refusal of pensions. No one in Germany thought that in order to combat the past, its representatives must be made personally defenceless and economically impotent. Outwardly it was nothing more than a purely political reversal, borne aloft by representatives of pure humanitarianism; a humane revolution is necessarily a semi-revolution. This was probably the deepest error of the men of 1848. Revolution is battle and carries the principle of force into the formation of the State. The princes had always made their wars ruthlessly without regard either to other peoples or to their own. The German democratic movement of 1848 wished to achieve a gentle victory. No historian will reproach the leaders with shedding too little blood; there are other ways of removing opponents. The Revolution of 1848 did not perceive them or took no note of them. The leaders must have known their opponents well enough, but did nothing to cripple their activity or to replace them in their posts by followers of the new order. The Frankfort central power could have chosen people in whom they could have confidence; but the old particularistic bureaucratic machine continued to rattle untroubled on its way. There were martyrs enough from the Revolution of 1830 and the Wars of Liberation. Certainly they were elected to the Frankfort Parliament — Ernst Moritz Arndt, Jahn, Uhland, Eisenmann, Sylvester Jordan — but they had very little voice in affairs. The young revolutionaries suffered from the German fault of overtrustfulness. They took no revenge; the patriotic and liberty-loving citizens saw the principal danger in the Jacobins, Social-Revolutionaries, and Communists.

Naturally, there was much malicious joy over the fall of the mighty; the lack of talent for quick, sharp action was compensated for by a tremendous gift for scolding: grumbling, criticism, speculations as to how it could have been better done, frittered away the urge to action. Curiously enough, this quarrelsome criticism rapidly turned from the old to expend its force against the new leaders. The new men may have had their weaknesses; but they were mercilessly exposed. The moment anyone rose to the top, he was attacked with embittered jealousy; Welcker, Heinrich von Gagern, Robert Blum, Friedrich Hecker — the same fate overtook them all. This was the reverse side of the medal of the conscientious revolution of 1848; it destroyed its own children. The Revolution had practically talked itself to death by the time the Counter-Revolution was on the march. The people's leaders had only a momentary authority; they had continually to fight for it; their weaknesses were those of the people themselves and therefore unforgivable. Public opinion was particularly resentful if the new men profited economically from their work. Anyone who accepted a government position with a fixed income, like Karl Mathy or Wilhelm Jordan, was already half a traitor. Heinrich von Gagern was so sensitive on this point that it was necessary absolutely to force upon him the salary accompanying the post of President of the Frankfort Parliament by passing a law that there could be no refusal of this salary. A healthy desire to see clean hands in public affairs was thus so exaggerated as to lead to pure absurdity. For the bureaucratic apparatus remained, just for this reason, practically unchanged.

Thus the humanitarian State, as the March movement dreamed of it, could not come into being. Men longed for action and feared it at the same time. When the big speeches were over, there was remarkable modesty in deeds and also a certain hesitation. The old layer of officialdom presented a very solid front in comparison. It did not glitter, it did not trifle, it was something in itself and had no need to become anything different. When these people accused the democratic leaders of wanting to snatch office, of vanity and who knows what else, there was scarcely anyone who thought to rebuff the questioner by asking where these noblemen, these property-owners, these manufacturers had come by their fortunes. Most of the new people were poor and suffered from poverty; they therefore hesitated between shyness and excited claims; they had talent, good sense, patriotism, a feeling for what was right; they turned everything into debate, believed they could convince the majority and carried motions; they thought they could alter German realities by a new Constitution, by new laws. It was an honourable undertaking, but unfortunately the mass of the public soon grew tired of it. There was not enough going on, it was not rapid, not dramatic, not wild enough. The loud-mouthedness which sprang up by the side of the noble pioneers of a new justice, awakened in the mass of the public a respect for what had been; pity and sympathy for fallen greatness is also a good trait of the German nature; only a clever twisting of contemporary events was necessary to weld a new loyalty, in exercising which the people thought themselves mighty fine fellows and true as steel. It was just those who had always been despised and ill-treated by the old powers who now made use of the opportunity to get a little nearer to the throne, without running any great danger and so to gain social and economic advantages. The nobles had always had a certain independence; unquestioning devotion was to be the characteristic of this new class of citizen.

The Reform movement had tried to be just to everyone, a political point of view must never anticipate the judgment of history. Will to righteousness made these men self-righteous. This roused their political opponents to absolute hatred. The Republicans, the Social-Revolutionaries, the Communists had the active courage to be unjust; but only minorities followed their lead.

The Counter-Revolution certainly had more courage to be unjust. There was no question of asking whether blood might be shed or property destroyed; there was no need to seize the means of power; the Counter-Revolution had all that was necessary. If the popular movement in North Germany, except in Berlin, seemed somewhat lacking in temperament, the Counter-Revolution was undoubtedly more emotional. Religion, patriotism, morality, loyalty to the traditional ruling house proceeded to the attack. The Revolution had branded only Metternich as a criminal; the Counter-Revolution branded a whole social class as rogues and vagabonds. When the vanquished marched out of Rastatt, the Prince of Prussia turned away. He did not want to see "such people." The Revolution had built up a legend of its own pre-history; the Counter-Revolution now wrote the legend of the nature of this democratic movement and thus exercised a decisive influence upon two German generations. The Revolution had taken care to make no martyrs; the Counter-Revolution had no such scruples. Ordinary courts competed with courts-martial. The feeling of justice, so sensitive at this time, was once more deeply wounded by a whole series of political trials.

Jacob Burckhardt said power was an evil thing. There is something worse than power. Power is, above all, fickle. It must be won and manifested afresh from day to day. Only use can keep it bright and keen. It serves only those who grasp it firmly. Woe to them who possess it and do not use it, for it will turn against them. This was the experience of the German citizen of 1848; the measure of logical retribution which he had not in himself, was visited upon him with interest by the Counter-Revolution. The humanitarian, the decent citizen, the cosmopolitan dialectician, had no more to say. The world had shown that it was not beautiful and pure as the classic form, nor joyous and brightly-coloured like an intellectual romantic play. A dashing age usurped the scene, impudent and coarse, unashamed, inclined to mockery and brutality. Certainly no political movement could be suppressed entirely by police and the courts; there were more subtle measures and these had a decisive effect. The "people," it was said, had proved themselves to be insolent, avaricious, rough, and treacherous; they needed control and they should have it. Arrogance and contempt of mankind, the ancient vices of ruling classes, now went disguised as the art of protective government. . . .

Bismarck is a complete contrast to the democratic movement of 1848: the popular movement wanted to win the dukedoms of Schleswig and Holstein as a German petty state — Bismarck simply annexed them. The democratic movement wished to free the Poles, or at least to secure the rights of the Polish people within the Prussian State — Bismarck sacrificed the idea of Polish independence for the sake of Prussian friendship and began the Prussianization of the Poles; the 1848 movement wished as a majority to see the Little-German democratic empire of the King of Prussia preserving the petty states, suppressing Prussian State egotism, and, as a minority, wished for decided unitarism in place of particularistic federalism — Bismarck created a Great-Prussian Empire firmly bound to authority, he annexed a number of Central German states, but left the South Germans to themselves, especially Bavaria; he took over universal suffrage for the empire, but in Prussia and therefore also in a number of allied states, he prevented free development, in the interests of the dynasties and the ruling classes. . . .

The new never entirely destroyed the

old. The German is not good at destruction. Even after the founding of Bismarck's empire, German unity was a foreign political and economic reality, but not a spiritual experience of the people as a whole. This is still more true of the political forms of the Weimar republic period. The demands arising from them will always lead us back to 1848. He who is not certain what to do will certainly not find that history informs him. But he whose will is clearly set to certain aims ahead can search the past and find an answer there. Every century since the sixteenth has brought severe civil struggles in Germany. The old German lust of battle found vent in wars between the individual states every time a quarrel arose. Not until the German Confederation of 1815 was there any peacefulness, at the cost of freedom. When the people of 1848 arose, everyone once more fought against everyone else; but the struggle did not come fully to a head. To this extent the year 1866 represents the late realization of everything that had been neglected or could not be achieved by the better way of understanding. The year 1866 is a secular epoch — it was thrust into the background by the brilliance and fulfilment of the year 1870–71, but historically speaking, it weighed almost more heavily.

Nations have the primeval right to throw off foreign oppression. They also have the primeval right so to shape the State that it is ruled by a class of leaders so fitted for the task that the working people are taught to be contented. A great deal of force has been used in Germany — formerly it was mostly the slaves, peasants, citizens, working-men, who bore the brunt. The peace-loving cosmopolitan, too, may be turned into a world-revolutionary by the narrow-minded opposition of those in power. Revolution is not a sin. With the year 1848, a new era of revolutions began, which is not yet at an end. Fichte already sought the Revolution which Napoleon had ruined. Just as Bismarck in 1866 asked an indemnity from the Prussian people's representatives, so should the whole military-bureau-

cratic epoch of Imperial Germany have begged a timely indemnity from the idea of the free democratic State. The right to revolution finds its only limitations in the degree of talent available to carry it through and create a new State. Formerly revolutions and wars were strictly divided. The danger of revolution was parried by declaring war, and lost wars usually ended in revolution. Today pointing of war and revolution is seen as an identical threat, pointing in different directions, achieved by the same means. Every revolution, too, is a technical fighting problem. In 1848, fighting was done simultaneously with antiquated weapons, such as the barricade system and the volunteer principle, and with very modern weapons, such as the utilization of means of transport and the organization of news. Wars and revolutions seem to be growing more and more to resemble one another; the revolutions have learned from the wars the idea of universal arming of the people, as was repeatedly done in 1848. War learnt terrorism from revolution. We know that the reform of the Prussian Army in the 'sixties can be traced back to the attitude of the Prussian Landwehr or reserve troops, in 1848–49, which, in many places, felt themselves as militia rather than as tools of authority.

The popular movement of 1848, the strongest motive in which was the national urge, ended with the conviction that nationalism and internationalism are contrary poles. But always, ever since the days of feudalism, Europe has been a unit. Have not Kant and Goethe influenced England; Hegel, France; Nietzsche, Italy; Marx and Engels, Russia, to the greatest extent? There is no isolation. Today we see very plainly that a fruitful and peaceful international life is only possible between democratic nations, ripened, grown peaceful, nationally satisfied. The history of Germany as a nation and as a form of State and society is not yet complete. It may be carried on by fresh revolutions, but not necessarily. There is no danger of revolution which cannot be banned by reforms and wise statesmanship. The Revolution of 1848, trodden underfoot by the Counter-Revolution, was not dead. It sat in the Eternal Paulskirche of Greater Germanism and waited for the hour of re-birth. Doubtless it is still sitting there to this day. The old cannot and will not return. But the patriotism of 1848, in its purity and its resolve, is the immortal ally in all future struggles of the German nation.

WHY THE REVOLUTION OF 1848 FAILED

WILLIAM EBENSTEIN

Born in Austria in 1910 and educated at the universities of Vienna, London, and Wisconsin, William Ebenstein has been professor of politics at Princeton University since 1949, specializing in the history of political thought. During the Second World War, Ebenstein turned aside briefly from his studies of political theory to write *The German Record: A Political Portrait,* in which he endeavored to interpret the German national character on the basis of the historical development of Germany. The thesis of the book is that the mass of the German people, not only Hitler and his Nazi followers, must be held responsible for the wrongs which Germany committed against other nations and peoples during the war, and Ebenstein points to the German record throughout history as proof of this concept. In the following excerpt dealing with the revolutions of 1848, Ebenstein contradicts Valentin's laudatory account of the Frankfort National Assembly, denigrating that parliamentary body for its inability to deal with practical political problems. Again in contradiction to Valentin, he emphasizes how thorough was the defeat of German liberalism in 1848.

THIS QUESTION will be raised as long as German liberalism is a hope rather than a reality. The easiest, and most misleading, answer would be to turn to racialism. According to that theory, the failure of German liberalism in 1848 was due to the innate incapacity of the German people (or, better even, "race") to achieve and appreciate freedom. The advocates of this view overlook the fact that the Scandinavian nations, even more purely Germanic than the Germans, have shown themselves quite capable of freedom and self-government. The Dutch and German-speaking Swiss also point to the fallacy of any racialist explanations of this problem.

The concrete, historical reasons which explain the failure of German liberalism in 1848 are manifold: First, the question of national unity interfered with the social issues of class structure and class influence.

England and France had been united for centuries before their social revolutions developed to maturity and success. In both of these countries a powerful middle class had gained increasing momentum and power within the framework of a united national state. In Germany, on the other hand, the middle class was broken up by dozens of sovereign states. In this fragmentation lay one of the most important sources of paralysis when the middle classes were confronted with the need for concerted action. Separatism of the non-Russian nationalities in the Russian bourgeois revolution of March, 1917, and Catalan and Basque regionalism in the Spanish bourgeois revolution of 1931 were no small causes of the ultimate collapse of liberalism in both cases.

The problem of national unity was closely connected with that of the position of foreign nationalities in Germany. The

French national state was solidly French. To the extent that a foreign people, the Irish, were dominated by the English, the internal English situation was continuously complicated. As long as the Irish issue was a monkey wrench thrown into English politics, English liberalism was in constant danger. Later, the problem reappeared in the wider implications of imperialism for home politics. The alternative was this: either the authoritarianism of imperial government would eventually destroy the liberal democracy at home or the domestic habits of self-government would liberalize the empire. The latter alternative eventually prevailed in England.

German liberalism was confronted in 1848 with the difficulties of a nation organized in thirty-nine separate sovereign states. In addition, the problem of the non-German nationalities had to be faced. This issue presented itself in a twofold manner: Some German lands, such as Hanover and Holstein, were ruled by foreign princes (the kings of England and Denmark, respectively). The Germans of Austria were ruled by the Hapsburgs, a German dynasty. But the Austrian empire was a sea of non-German nations in which the German-speaking group formed but a small island. Conversely, non-German nationalities were ruled by German princes. Prussia with her millions of Polish subjects and Austria with her tens of millions of non-German groups (Magyars, Czechs, Slovaks, Croats, Poles, Italians) constituted thorny problems obstructing the creation of a free and united Germany.

German liberalism had to deal with the subject foreign nationalities before it had achieved power. The Holy Roman Empire had wrestled with this issue for centuries without providing a satisfactory solution. It was no easy task, therefore, for German liberalism, cautiously groping forward, to find a way out of this dilemma. The weight of a thousand-year-old tradition militated against the bestowal of independence upon the non-German nationalities and their exclusion from the Reich.

The Polish question in Prussia contained enough explosive force to "tear the whole German nation asunder into two camps." As in most other questions, the democratic convictions of the small minority of the Left were overwhelmed by the nationalist chauvinism of the Center and Right groups. The Poles, like the Czechs, Hungarians and Italians, were refused national independence on the ground of the superiority of German Kultur. In their megalomania of race superiority, the majority of the Germans of 1848 seemed in no way different from the Germans of 1918 and 1933. As late as February, 1918, Gustav Stresemann ridiculed in the Reichstag Polish demands for independence.

The German middle classes grew in a period of economic development different from that which had favored the expansion, economic and political, of the French and British middle classes. The classical bourgeois economy of eighteenth-century France and England was based on small-scale enterprise, generally owned and managed by one family. Owner, manager and worker were united in one person or one family. The passionate pleas of early political individualism in France, Britain and the United States sought to translate the theory and practice of economic individualism into the political sphere. The Jeffersonian vision of America is perhaps the purest expression of a commonwealth made up of men and women who serve no masters economically or politically, and who rule none but themselves.

With the rapid technological development of the late eighteenth and early nineteenth centuries the nature of free enterprise changed. The farmer, bulwark of economic and political individualism, was increasingly replaced in his relative position in the national economy by the manufacturer, businessman and industrial worker. Industrialization as the process of relative deagrarianization of the national economy created threats to self-government which still await a satisfactory solution.

This tendency was accelerated by another fact. Progress in technology led to concentration of capital, owing to large-scale methods of production and distribution. This concentration of capital entailed an increased influence of the state or of a small class of capitalists, while a new class developed which owned no capital and could sell only one good: human labor.

This was the historical situation confronting the German middle classes. For reasons mentioned before (such as the Thirty Years' War, the decline of Continental trade following the discovery of America, political separatism), the growth of the German middle classes lagged behind the British, French and Dutch middle classes by about one hundred and fifty years. When the German bourgeoisie entered upon its path of economic expansion, small-scale enterprise was no longer technologically efficient. Large-scale enterprise led to concentration of capital in the hands of a few — opposed by a new propertyless class of agricultural and industrial workers. When the German middle classes waged their decisive struggle for political power in the eighteen-forties, they were confronted by a new situation in European history. They set out to fight privilege, oppression and political monopoly of the aristocratic and feudal groups, but they themselves were already seriously attacked in the rear by the revolutionary groups of the industrial working classes.

The year 1848 saw not only the attempt of the German middle classes to establish a "constitution" directed against irresponsible power above. The same year also witnessed the publication of the *Communist Manifesto,* clarion call of the revolutionary proletariat. In the seventeenth and eighteenth centuries, the British and French middle classes had to fight on only one front: against the privileged classes above, without being simultaneously menaced by a threat from the lower classes. The Levellers represented the Communist or, at least, Left wing of the Puritan Revolution in seventeenth-century England. However, they were so weak, economically and politi-

cally, that they could be easily suppressed and passed off as political "freaks" not to be taken seriously. The French Revolution witnessed some Communist uprisings. But the working class was so small and insignificant at that early period of economic evolution that it could be easily controlled. The political weakness was also reflected in the immaturity and confusion of Communist and Socialist thought at that time. By 1848, on the other hand, communism and socialism had become political facts.

The *Communist Manifesto,* written by Karl Marx and Friedrich Engels upon the request of the "Communist League" at the congress in London in November, 1847, opens with these famous phrases: "A ghost is haunting Europe — the ghost of Communism. All the powers of old Europe have allied themselves in a holy hunt against this ghost: Pope and Czar, Metternich and Guizot, French radicals and German police agents. Where is the party in opposition that has not been decried as communistic by its opponents in power?"

The German middle classes thus waged war on two fronts: against the feudal Junkers and absolute kings above and against the working class below. Two-front wars can be as disastrous in social as in military history. That was the deepest cause of the failure of German liberalism in 1848–1849. For the first time in modern history a situation of this kind presented itself to a rising middle class. Since then, similar strategical situations of social and political warfare have developed in other countries. Each case has, in broad terms, repeated the German experience. The Russian bourgeois revolution of March, 1917, and the Spanish bourgeois revolution of 1931 are both notable instances of the failure of middle-class movements that have to fight on two fronts in the hour of their grasp for power. The struggle against the old upper classes in the name of political liberty and equality was in both cases, as in that of the German revolution of 1848–1849, perverted by the anxiety to maintain economic inequality and privilege against the lower classes. Wilhelm

Riehl, one of the founders of German sociology, referred in 1852 to the German Socialists as "the common enemy," against whom all classes of society had to unite in common defense.

In our own time, the temporary defeat of French liberal institutions in 1940 was in no mean way due to the openly expressed preference of men of property in France that "Hitler was better than Blum." Britain was on the verge of national calamity in 1940 because the blind fear of socialism had prevented an Anglo-Russian alliance in the prewar years. Appeasement of the Axis powers by Britain and the United States in the years 1931–1939 was too complex a policy to be explained by a single factor. Undoubtedly, war weariness of the masses and false conceptions of pacifism played into the hands of the Axis alliance of loot. But there is no question that the persistence of influential groups in looking upon Nazi-Fascism as a bulwark against Bolshevism was one of the decisive factors responsible for the eventual disasters of appeasement, culminating in Dunkerque and Pearl Harbor. The poison of intellectual appeasement had eaten so deeply into the body politic of some Western nations that it was seriously suggested that not only could the democracies "do business with Hitler," but that Nazism was the "wave of the future!"

What about the attitude of other countries toward the German revolution of 1848? The Germans in the United States, refugee greenhorns as well as immigrant old-timers, actively supported liberal revolutionary movements in Germany in the eighteen-forties. No Fritz Kuhns and no Bundists at that time! This influence of German-Americans was especially felt in southwestern Germany. A revolutionary poster, distributed in Baden in 1847, urged the creation of a free country "like America." A pamphlet was circulated early in 1848 in Wiesbaden which contained the following appeal: "Look to the thousands of our brethren of all classes who annually emigrate to North America. As soon as they have set foot on the soil of the free country, they are ripe for republicanism. As we all know, they deem themselves fortunate to live under that form of government." Before the revolution of 1848 a German translation of the Constitution of the United States was brought out in Stuttgart, and immediately became an important source of liberal-republican inspiration.

This historical tie between German democracy and the United States was even more accentuated after the initial successes of the revolution. When the National Assembly met in the St. Paul's Church in Frankfort, the President of the United States was the only head of state who greeted it officially. Likewise, the United States was the only nation which granted official recognition to the new government set up by the National Assembly. England and France, on the other hand, did not grant full recognition to the diplomatic representatives of the National Assembly. The conduct of both countries at that time contributed to lessening the prestige of German liberalism at home and abroad. They failed to see, as they failed later in 1918, that by encouraging German progressive forces, even revolution, they would render a service not only to the German people and mankind, but to their own national interests as well.

This does not mean, of course, that the failure of liberal democracy in Germany in 1848, or in 1918, was due to the faults and errors of the Western nations, especially France, Britain and the United States. Anti-Nazi Germans like to emphasize this argument in explaining and justifying the weakness and failure of democracy in Germany. While there is a certain amount of truth in the argument, it can be stretched too far. After all, the English went through two rather decisive revolutions in the seventeenth century without outside aid or sympathy — least of all from the Germans. The French and American peoples successfully fought their great revolutions in the eighteenth century — without, again, any aid or sympathy from the Germans. In the case of France, the Germans tried to crush the Revolution by outright military intervention and invasion. In the case of the American Revolution, the Hessians did not exactly speed up its success. The nineteenth-century revolutions in France, Italy and Latin America succeeded without substantial aid from outside. Finally, in the twentieth century, revolutionary republican movements have triumphed in Mexico, China and Russia without outside help, and often, in fact, against the hostility of powerful foreign nations.

THE YEAR 1848 IN GERMAN HISTORY: REFLECTIONS ON A CENTENARY

FRIEDRICH MEINECKE

Friedrich Meinecke is the most illustrious German historian of the twentieth century. An outstanding teacher, Meinecke was also chief editor of the *Historische Zeitschrift,* the foremost organ of German historical scholarship, from 1898 until the Nazis forced his resignation in 1936. After the Second World War, Meinecke resumed seminar teaching at the University of Berlin and was a founder of the Free University in West Berlin, of which he became the first rector and, until his death (in 1954, at the age of 92), honorary rector. Early in his career Meinecke became fascinated with the problem of the conflict between *Geist* and *Macht,* between idea and power, endeavoring to interpret German history in this light, and especially to bring about a synthesis between the ethical and political elements in the German "soul," as symbolized by Goethe and Bismarck respectively. Although he came from a background of Prussian conservatism, the First World War shattered his illusions regarding power politics, and he became a reluctant democrat, giving increasing support to the Weimar Republic. When he emerged from retirement after the Second World War, Meinecke attempted a final interpretation of the German "catastrophe" in terms of the antimony between political and private ethics, the study of which had dominated his historical scholarship. This same approach is applied in the following excerpt from an article written on the centenary of the 1848 revolutions.

Tᴴᴇ ᴘᴏᴘᴜʟᴀʀ uprising of the March Days of 1848 in Berlin, superficially viewed, remained an episode, and the men who were fighting for progress along various lines failed, and were bound to fail, in their aims. The German revolution, said Friedrich Engels in his instructive articles of 1851–52 (which he published in America above the signature of Karl Marx), was a necessity, but its temporary suppression was similarly unavoidable. We shall still have to substantiate this, but must turn our gaze first upon the Berlin revolution, and upon the positive comment which it may offer for our contemporary historical situation. Yet for this too it is necessary to search somewhat deeper.

We must set before ourselves today more sharply than before, the problem of critical alternatives in the history of Germany, in order to gain a deeper insight into the infinitely complex web of her dark destiny. The natural task of Germany in the nineteenth century was not only to achieve unification, but also to transmute the existing authoritarian state (*Obrigkeitsstaat*) into commonwealth (*Gemeinschaftsstaat*). To that end, the monarchial-authoritarian

From Friedrich Meinecke, "The Year 1848 in German History: Reflections on a Centenary," *The Review of Politics,* X (1948), pp. 475–488. By permission of *The Review of Politics,* Notre Dame, Indiana.

structure had to be made elastic — if possible, through peaceful reform — so that the result would be an active and effective participation of all strata of society in the life of the state. This was imperatively demanded by the new configuration which was in process within the German society, and which was undermining the former aristocratic foundations of the authoritarian monarchy. An upper middle class arose, the lower middle class increased in large strides, and the beginnings of the industrial proletariat in the middle of the century gave notice of its mighty growth to come. Now, the task of reorganizing and harmonizing within a new commonwealth a people in social transition, bursting with vitality, remained largely unfulfilled, although many liberal and democratic concessions were granted by the old authorities. Which then were the decisive points in this development? When were possibilities first seen, attempts made or frustrated, which could have brought Germany forward upon the path to the commonwealth?

I see, above all, three such moments. The first occurs toward the end of the Prussian era of reform, in the year 1819 — the year of the Carlsbad Decrees — when with the dismissal of Wilhelm von Humboldt and Boyen, their most fruitful constitutional projects were also buried, and the authoritarian and militaristic principle triumphed in Prussia. The second crisis, when this principle once more won out in the end, was the year 1848. And the third point of decision was the Prussian era of conflict and the year 1866, which, while seeing some progress made toward satisfying the desire for national unity and strength, allowed the liberal and democratic ideas only a partial or apparent success. For it separated the way of the upsurging popular movements from the authoritarian-militaristic citadel of the entire national life.

Of these three fundamental decisions of the nineteenth century, the first was fought out in the more restricted circle of the ruling class itself, between high-minded and farsighted statesmen on the one hand

and a monarch of limited understanding on the other. The third crisis developed as a duel between the liberal upper middle class and Bismarck, in which that tremendously skilful campaigner understood how to win over at last a large part of the opposition. At no time in the years before 1866, was the weapon of a revolution seriously considered by Bismarck's progressive antagonists; they were fearful of it, in accordance with the instincts of an upper bourgeoisie. The second crisis — that of 1848 — offers therefore a unique, and for us today, a moving spectacle: here the whole people, not Prussians alone, but Germans of every class, stepped into the arena, and an actual revolution came about.

Revolutions, fearful as the invasion of irrational forces may be, or turn out to be, have in certain cases their deep historical justification. Such was the case in Germany, and especially in Prussia, in the year 1848. Admittedly the old order, now attacked by the revolution, was not in all aspects characterized by decay or ossification. The *Biedermeierzeit* with its lovely spiritual flowering had gone before. The Zollverein, since 1833 a work of the Prussian bureaucracy, had made secure the indispensable preconditions for the rise of modern economic forces, and thereby also for the social transformation from which the revolution itself had sprung. The psychopathic romanticist who now sat on the throne of the Hohenzollerns was himself inspired with a deep love for German civilization (*Deutschtum*), and was at some pains to bring about a German unity in its own way. But this way contradicted most sharply the urgent needs of the time. It was upon illusions that he based his attempts to reform the wretched organization of the German Bund and to fulfill the promise of a constitution (made in 1815) by the assembling of the united provincial diets in 1847. For the strongly aristocratic composition of these provincial estates, and the narrow powers which were all that the king would concede to them, were completely inadequate to satisfy the claims of popular representation which grew out of the process of social change. And in everyday life one felt everywhere the old absolutist-militarist police state, unbroken in spite of the isolated concessions to liberalism which the king, giving with one hand and rescinding with the other, might make. But behind the reaction against his personal and self-contradictory rule, and behind all individual grievances, there stood as a deepest source of discontent and feeling that the Prussian military and Junker state must be reorganized from the ground up — that the old authoritarian state must give way to a new commonwealth.

In fact this emotion, spurring on toward revolution, was not actually evoked but only powerfully stimulated, by the February revolution in France and the scattered revolts that were flaring up throughout Germany and even in Metternich's own Vienna. The remarkable circumstance that everywhere they succeeded at once, without encountering resistance, would demonstrate that the moral position of the rulers themselves was already noticeably shaken, that they no longer possessed an unquestioning and naive faith in the viability of the old order. Such a faith was necessary, if the governments were to use against the revolution the physical instrumentalities of power, still amply available to them. When later they realized that these resources were still at their disposal, the authorities did not hesitate to act accordingly, and to suppress the revolution with reaction. But as things were in March, 1848, they all, as Frederick William IV later expressed it, "lay flat on their bellies."

He, the king himself, most of all. And this in spite of the fact that he had actually launched, on the 18th of March, the physical auxiliaries of his power — his faithful army — successfully against the people's barricades in Berlin. Yet on the very next day, he permitted, through his own order, these troops — though undefeated — to abandon the inner city which they had conquered, and thereby exposed the person of the king to the severest of humiliations at

the hands of the rebels. Let us leave aside entirely the tangled complexity of these events, which have been investigated time and again, and emphasize only this. So feeble and contradictory a policy could not have been conducted by any prince, who, with a pure and undiminished faith in his old world, was simply defending it against a new. This new world had already to some degree insinuated itself, secretly and unsuspected, into his own thinking, distracting and weakening his power for effective action. Sooner or later the new was bound to win out, in spite of many setbacks to come, and to replace the authoritarian state by some form of democracy.

Such an interpretation may be justified, as we look back over the whole century that separates us from the year 1848, and as we think of the task now before us — the task of casting aside all relics of the authoritarian state (of which the Third Reich was, in fact, but a malignant outgrowth), and building up a sound and vigorous democracy. The easy victory — to be sure, not a military but a political and psychological victory — by which the street-fighting in Berlin prevailed over the old military monarchy, suggested symbolically that the latter's downfall was written in the stars; that one day the sovereignty of the people would become a reality. But, at the same time, it was no more than a symbol. For the new world was as yet quite untested and immature, and the old world still possessed many unexploited resources — even the chance of remaining victorious for some time to come. Bismarck and his work, after all, had sprung from it, at once magnificent and ephemeral. But let us now mark clearly the indications of that immaturity in which the new world of democracy then continued to find itself.

First a glance at Berlin. The men on the barricades of the 18th of March certainly fought bravely and fiercely, more fiercely than the Parisians before them had fought on the 24th of February. Such was the opinion of the Frenchman Circourt, who had come to Berlin as the representative of the new republican government, and had witnessed both engagements. But was it really the whole of the Berlin populace that stood behind the fighting or accompanied it with good wishes? Pastor Bodelschwingh, son of the minister whose task it was to pass on the royal command for retreat on the 19th of March, wrote in 1902: "We youngsters were running about on the streets that Sunday morning (March 19). With the uprising repelled, there reigned a joyful mood among the greater part of our population; everywhere from the houses the troops were plied with food." Of course, most of the individual bits of evidence which we possess concerning the 18th and 19th of March, are colored to some extent by the sympathies of the witness, and so this testimony of Bodelschwingh should not be taken too literally either. But even less does it deserve to be entirely discarded. And a glance at the general attitude of the German upper middle class in the years 1848–49 reveals all the more clearly that large sections of this class were still greatly desirous of tranquillity, and continued to be loyal to the old authorities.

It is necessary to go more deeply into these questions, in order to explain the paradoxical fact that the German revolution of 1848 could everywhere succeed so easily at first, and then in the sequence of events be overthrown with comparatively little effort. To understand this, the character, attitudes, and moral habits of the German people as it was at that time, and those of the various social strata within it, must be taken into consideration. And our contemporary need to attain to an inner relationship with this first attempt at German democracy gives this problem all the more importance.

The German people had only just emerged from the years of thinking, writing, and striving. But the thinking and dreaming continued likewise within the framework of new achievements and new desires. This ideological groundswell is common to all parties and classes within the German people, from Frederick Wil-

liam IV and his devout Christian-German friends – the extremists of reaction – all the way to the extremists of revolution: the men whose forceful minds conceived the Communist Manifesto of 1848, Karl Marx and Engels. For did not Hegel live on with them – a Hegel in reverse and yet preserved (*aufgehoben*)? Was it not true of both these thinkers, who claimed to regard all ideologies as merely secondary efforts of fundamental economic forces, that in them there came to life something distinctly ideological – an unqualified belief in the determining power of the laws of development – set up at a time when they themselves found only a tiny handful of followers? In any case, we ought no more gainsay the strong impulse of idealism which worked in these men, than that operating in Dahlmann and Gagern – the champions of the liberal nation-state – or in the brothers Gerlach, defenders of a divinely ordained corporative state. The German revolution of 1848, admittedly, shows not only an all-pervading spirit of idealism, which often outstripped reality and became ideological. It also brought to bear what in actual effect was more powerful – the reality itself, the massive and elemental interests of individuals and social groups. And, because it *was* a revolution, it likewise saw the release of base passions, and outrages of all kinds, perpetrated by the Right as well as by the Left. But if 1848 is compared with other revolutions – and particularly with the most ignominious of all revolutions, that of 1933 – it can be stated that the factor of human depravity played a comparatively insignificant role. This must not be obscured by the fact that the extremist parties took pleasure in accusing one another of disgraceful conduct. Theirs were for the most part "atrocity stories." Neither was there anything which could be termed a "brutalized soldiery," nor were the barricades and the free corps of Hecker and Struve manned by a mere "mob." The German people, considered as a whole, kept in those days to a comparatively high moral level.

It must be admitted that their level of

life no longer possessed the spiritual grandeur of the age of Goethe. This decline was unavoidable in any case, since the urgent task of establishing a new political and social way of life compressed men into mass or group patterns, and made it more difficult for the individual to gather within himself the creative force from which proceeds all great culture. But what mattered now was, whether this people would prove to possess the maturity, the strength, the insight and steadfastness, that its new task demanded. Certainly, as we have noted, it was written in the stars that one day the new world would triumph over the old, popular sovereignty over the authoritarian state. But could the victory be achieved at this juncture? The fact that the revolution failed does not necessarily prove that the people were not ready; this may have been due to the coincidence of accidental factors. How bitter were the complaints, in the very midst of events, that just such a personality as Frederick William IV should have been for the revolution its "man of destiny" — a man who had actually, out of weakness, bowed before it at the outset, but who had then stubbornly resisted it; and by his refusal of the imperial office on April 3, 1849, had allowed the nation's call for the creation of the liberal nation-state to die away. Certainly another man in his place could have attempted another and possibly more propitious solution of the German problem. Then, however, the success of the attempt would once more have depended, in the last analysis, upon the world situation. This aspect of the problem we shall take up later. Suffice it now to ask again: was the German people really prepared for the task ahead?

Basic attributes and historical experiences, working together, had made the German people parochial, not only outwardly but inwardly as well, to a degree hardly equalled in any other nation of Europe. The princely territorial state, multiplied a hundredfold to the point where it exhibited absurd extremes of dwarfishness, depended everywhere upon a landed gentry which served

the state and, in return, held sway over those beneath them. All this had mingled with the German bloodstream and had rendered the German people obedient and lacking in political self-reliance. In this very multiplication of authority, we see the chief means by which the mentality of the authoritarian state penetrated so deeply into the pores of German life.

One need only compare this with the development of England and France, where the royal absolutism — in England short-lived anyhow — had indeed helped to create a unified nation, but had never been able to instil so lasting and thoroughgoing a habit of obedience, as had the multiplicity of small German principalities. How far an original or native trait had helped to bring this about, can only be conjectured. Was it perhaps the spirit of fealty described by Tacitus? But the example of the Germans in Switzerland and their historical development since the Middle Ages indicates that there were other potentialities of a political nature inherent in the German character. Free of princely and therefore of rigid rule, subject only to patrician and — by the same token — more pliable authority, Switzerland was enabled to develop the native democratic tenet of her original cantons into the governing principle of her commonwealth, and thus to build upon historical foundations a modern democracy. No, the German need not submit to any fatalistic dread that because he is a German, he may for ever and ever be condemned to the habits of servility implanted by the authoritarian state. But it takes time, much time, again to tear free of it. Then too, this state has borne the German people, along with evil fruits, many and varied benefits, and thus fashioned much of ethical value that might well be carried over into the new world of the democratic commonwealth.

Good and evil alike, then, grew out of this disposition toward obedience, whose origin may well be placed primarily in the political fragmentation referred to above. Even where a larger political entity was growing up, as in Prussia, the extreme insistence upon this subservient attitude brought out in a manner especially striking the contrast between its good and evil effects. Prussia was, indeed, a state with two souls: the one austere and narrow, withdrawing into itself; the other culturally alive, striving, in Boyen's phrase, toward a threefold alliance of *"Recht, Licht and Schwert."* This Prussia, at once forbidding and attractive, now exerted her influence upon the rest of Germany. But how much was this influence again bound to confuse and distract all the aims of revolutionary Germany! The singleness of revolutionary purpose which would have been necessary for a victory over the old order, was thus rendered at the outset far more difficult to achieve. Now the German people, breaking loose from its previous subservience, did indeed reach out tumultuously for unity, power and freedom — only to find itself divided anew when it sought to determine the methods by which these were to be accomplished. How deep was the disintegrating and paralyzing effect of the Austro-German (*grossdeutsche*) problem, which implied what to some seemed an avoidable, to others an inevitable sacrifice of a portion of their fellow-countrymen (*Brudersstamm*), and the break-up of a German national community; how strongly has this problem contributed to the negative result of the revolution! It is hardly necessary, in addition, to recall the particularism of the intermediate German states. In fact, it was not merely the egotistic instincts of the princes, of their court councillors and court provisioners, but particularistic tendencies as well, conscious or unconscious, in the people themselves, which came into conflict with the new yearning for unity.

These were the factors of secular growth, going back as far as the Middle Ages, which weakened and divided in advance any unified revolutionary purpose in the German people. To these, however, were now added problems of the most modern type, arising out of the new configuration of society. It is true that the one part of the people which now broke away from the old attitudes of obedience, and rose up against the authoritarian state and against the splintering apart of the nation, was agreed upon the demand for greater unity, power and freedom; but it fell out once again over the emphasis and interpretation to be placed upon one or another of these three words. For behind the national revolution there was unfolding a social revolution, a class struggle between the old, the newer, and the newest social strata. This fact was recognized most clearly at the time by Marx and Engels, the champions of the newest class — the industrial proletariat — which had only just arisen and was still by no means very numerous. Between this youngest and (as Marx and Engels dogmatically proclaimed) potentially most important class, and that which had ruled so far — the nobility and the higher bureaucracy — there lay the two clearly distinct divisions of the bourgeoisie: the upper and lower middle class. The first was of more recent origin; the other dated far back, though it was not nearly as old as the peasantry — who, together with agricultural laborers, still made up by far the preponderant majority of the people as a whole. (The committee on economic affairs of the Frankfurt Parliament estimated that they constituted virtually four-fifths of the total population at that time.) The share of the rural population in the revolution was certainly not unimportant, but created no particularly complicated issue for the fate of the revolution as a whole. Since a general land reform through the dismemberment of the large estates was not yet seriously envisioned, the agrarian problem of 1848 entailed only the casting-off of all remaining feudal encumbrances upon the peasant class and the peasant holdings. That was a comparatively simple task. Even conservative statesmen realized the necessity of solving this question at once, and when the peasants saw that steps in this direction were being taken or being planned, they calmed down again. They still shared sufficiently in the old habits of subservience, in any case. The young Bismarck could well consider using them as tools in the counter-revolution.

Side by side with the working class, the lower middle class provided most of the revolutionary energy. Craftsmen and workers formed the bulk of the fighters on the barricades. Had they not risen up, the revolution could not have achieved dynamic force at all, and all the idealists and theorists of the general movement (reaching into the upper middle class) would have remained officers without an army. There would have been no parliament in the Paulskirche, no draft for a German constitution with an hereditary Prussian emperor at its head. The craftsmen in Germany at that time were badly off. It was related in the Paulskirche that there was one small town with seventy tailors, of whom only seven were able to find employment. Some hardship was caused by guild restrictions which continued here and there. But a genuine guild spirit revived again, as is evidenced in the desperate struggle waged against the new machine by workers who were losing their livelihood, in the excesses committed by the waggoners against the railroads and by the boatsmen against the Rhine river steamers. These were all, in fact, merely symptoms of the basic feature of an age in which the machine, and the modern technology, had revolutionized the entire life of the western peoples, by creating new human masses and new, unsuspected and distressing situations among these masses.

In such a crisis, the old authoritarian stage proved unable for a long time to provide effective aid. Its officialdom was vacillating between benevolence and a narrow, pedantic attitude; its police a nuisance; its army — though possessed in the militia (*Landwehr*) of a more popular aspect — aroused bitter opposition by the arrogance and drill-ground manner of the regulars and their officers. Democracy as a cure for all these sufferings was the magic word that echoed through the ranks of the lower bourgeoisie — a class so quietist by nature

and so restless now. The working classes took up the same slogan, and added to it their own socialistic demands. The younger generation within the upper middle class in many places espoused the democratic cause with enthusiasm, and imbued it with the impulse of idealism. It was, to be sure, an exceedingly immature and primitive democracy of which these Germans dreamed, more a rejection of the old authoritarian state than a positive affirmation of the people's state resting upon a fully developed common spirit among all classes. The distrust and arrogance with which the various classes regarded one another, once more divided the very groups which had just made common cause against the old authorities. Let us illustrate this and other facts aforementioned, with certain experiences which the young Rudolf Virchow had in the March Days of Berlin.

Eight days before the 18th of March, he had returned from Upper Silesia, where he had been sent as a doctor to study the "hunger-typhus." He was indignant at the inability of the magistrates to take effective measures, and had long been convinced that the absolutist system of government was untenable. He assisted in the building of barricades on the 18th of March, and, armed with a pistol, placed himself at the one which blocked the Friedrichstrasse from the Taubenstrasse. Only six days later, he had to admit in a letter to his father: "Already there begins a reaction among the citizenry (Bourgeoisie) against the workers (the people). Already they are speaking of a rabble, already plans are being made for withholding equal distribution of political rights among the various groups in the nation." But, he added, the popular party would be alert and powerful, and would see to it "that no bourgeoisie should enjoy the fruits of a battle it had not waged."

One realizes here the closeness of the relationship between events in Berlin and the revolutions of 1830 and 1848 in France. But the problems of the German revolution were nevertheless much more complicated than those of the French uprisings. For the social revolution in Germany and its underlying class struggle was intertwined with the national revolution in a way which finally led to the failure of both. France no longer had need of a national revolution. She had long since achieved her unity, and her centralized power apparatus remained through one regime after another. In Germany both social equality and national consolidation were still to be achieved, with endless pains. And the need of the nation for unity and power was just as elemental and as deeply rooted in history as was the cry for domestic freedom and equality arising from those classes which the authoritarian state had so far kept down. Dahlmann in Frankfort even voiced the opinion that within the German desire for both power and freedom, the stronger impulse was now directed toward power, which had thus far been denied. The criminal excesses reached in our day by the need for power in Germany should by no means mislead us into condemning the elemental national craving of the men of '48. For theirs was a genuine hunger for something indispensable. Even Goethe had once acknowledged this fact, after the battle of Leipzig. "Art and science," he said to Luden, "are universal, and in view of these the bonds of nationality disappear. But the consolation they afford is but hollow comfort, and cannot replace the proud consciousness of belonging to a great, strong, feared and respected nation." Basically all the cravings of the year 1848 were permeated by kindred feelings and experiences. There was a general desire to leave behind the constricting and now intolerable bonds of the past, as one leaves behind a dark and airless dungeon. Just as the little man felt himself generally neglected and mistreated by the authoritarian state, so did the more cultivated German, who saw himself as a member of a great national community, and yet hemmed in by the irritating boundaries and the often ridiculous parochialism of thirty-eight greater or smaller authoritarian states. And equally neglected and thrust aside did he feel himself and his whole people to be within the entire body of European states.

All three of these desires [the liberal, the national, the European] were now, it was fondly hoped, to find their fulfilment through the Frankfurt National Assembly which, elected by universal and equal suffrage, convened on the 18th of May. Let us consider its social composition; it was noticeably different from what one might have expected as the result of the democratic suffrage imported from France. It contained no workers, only one genuine peasant, few members of the lower middle class, but many lawyers and judges — and, as is well known, many professors; nor were representatives of business and industry lacking. This indicates the still remaining respect of the lower for the upper strata of society, especially for the academically educated and in general for what is termed the upper bourgeoisie. But the same masses who now cast their votes for these people, were simultaneously in a state of unruly and turbulent commotion, which must necessarily have boded evil for the upper middle class interests and ideals. One had to rely on such an energetic thrust from below, in order to succeed at all to Frankfurt and the Paulskirche. But now it was a question, indeed, whether one could continue to employ these energies as indispensable weapons against the rulers, and yet keep them within limits, so as to guard against anarchy and the overturn of the social order.

In the last analysis, it was the danger of communism which appeared to threaten the whole bourgeoisie — not only the upper but the lower middle class as well. How real even the latter felt this threat to be, is exemplified by the bloody clash between the civil guard and the workers in Berlin on October 16, 1848. Communistic slogans and demands rang out from the enraged masses. A clearly conceived program, such as that of Marx and Engels, was in truth limited at first to the narrowest circles. But in a broader perspective, it appears that the very existence of a communist movement was perhaps decisive, or at least instrumental, in determining the course of events in 1848 — and, in the first instance, the attitude and policy of the Paulskirche. For it was in view of this communist threat that the middle class and its representation in the majority parties of the Paulskirche again and again were forced over toward the Right, toward some kind of compromise with the old authorities and their military resources. The same threat was instrumental in preventing the maintenance of a unified revolutionary purpose within the whole people, to which perhaps the government might at last have been forced to submit. We use the little word "perhaps," because historical questions of this sort cannot be treated like a mere problem in mathematics; because in every case where we have to consider the historical possibility of another kind of development than that which actually took place, an unknown "X" disturbs the calculation.

In any event, the parties of the majority — right and left center — which desired to establish a liberal, constitutional nation-state with an hereditary Prussian emperor as its head, found themselves in an extremely contradictory and precarious position. They needed the resources of a revolution just as much as those of a counter-revolution. But their position did not enable them to make full and unqualified use of either, without endangering the very basis of their undertaking. In their effort, however, to pursue a middle course and to bring both revolutionary and counter-revolutionary resources simultaneously or alternately into play, they incurred the danger, in turn, of becoming powerless themselves, and of seeing their cause wrecked against the forces of the stronger contender of the two — the counter-revolution. This, viewed as a whole, was to be their fate. Let us briefly point out here only the critical stages.

From France the signal had been given in February for the revolution; from France again the signal was given for the counter-revolution in June. In a terrible, three-day street battle, Cavaignac smashed the Paris workers. To be sure, the German middle class heaved a sigh of relief; but for them the ebbing of the revolutionary wave which now followed in Germany as well, was gain and loss alike — while for the reactionary forces of the authoritarian state, this turn constituted a clear gain. With the decline of communist fortunes, those of national liberalism sank as well.

This same dynamic course of events then unfolded during September. When the Prussian government concluded with Denmark the truce of Malmö, which seriously threatened the German claim to Schleswig, the aroused majority in the Paulskirche at first rejected it outright; but shortly thereafter, in view of the impracticable consequences of a refusal, the assembly, once more grown meek, ratified the agreement. And when an uprising from the Left now led to street fighting in Frankfurt itself and endangered the assembly, it was forced to turn for help to Prussian and Austrian troops (from the federal fortress at Mainz), in order to prevent a general landslide to the Left. Once more the fortunes of the authoritarian state rose, once more those of national liberalism sank. And they dropped still lower when the governments of Austria and Prussia, in October and November respectively, put down with their own military forces the rebellious democracy in Vienna and Berlin.

Under such circumstances was born the constitutional project of the Frankfurt National Assembly, culminating in the choice of the King of Prussia as hereditary emperor on March 28, 1849. Doubtless it was a proud achievement of the noblest aspiration toward national unity and freedom. But it lacked the basis of power which would have been necessary to put it through against the particularistic and reactionary forces of the authoritarian state. It was defeated at once when Frederick William IV, on April 3, 1849, refused to accept the new crown offered to him — a crown which in his view could appear only as a product of the revolution, a Danaean gift. And when the genuine revolution now reared its head again, and the disappointment which broad masses of the people experienced over the failure of Frankfurt exploded in the May uprisings in Pfalz and Baden, the equally disillusioned middle class — in order not to be engulfed altogether by revolution and the social upheaval that might follow — was forced once more, as in September, 1848, to lean on the authoritarian state. It had now exhausted its own role as an independent power factor, and had to be satisfied with the scant dole of liberal and national concessions which the insight of those who ruled Prussia might still be willing to grant. The May uprisings, on the other hand, were easily put down by Prussian troops. The fighters of the revolution, be they idealists of the urban educated class, little people of the lower bourgeoisie, or workers, proved completely inadequate to wage a

military campaign against the disciplined and dependable fighting force of the authoritarian state.

Upon these rocks was wrecked the German revolution. Only a unified revolutionary purpose, reconciling workers with bourgeoisie and upper with lower middle class, might have been able (as we have noted) to force another result and so to weaken the army's tradition of loyalty as to overthrow the old authorities. But the social transformation of the people, which brought on disruption within the entire middle class, had in fact made impossible from the first the growth of such a spirit of revolutionary unity. Without this social transformation, however — without a rising upper middle class, a lower middle class threatened with disintegration, and an aspiring working class — the revolution itself would have been impossible. Thus strangely and tragically intertwined were the inner necessity of this revolution and its inevitable failure. . . .

1848: SEED-PLOT OF HISTORY

L. B. NAMIER

Sir Lewis B. Namier's writings are known for their pungency and brilliance—and for having overturned accepted historical interpretations. From 1929 to 1931, Namier was Political Secretary of the Jewish Agency for Palestine, and he was Professor of Modern History at the University of Manchester from 1931 to 1953. His book, *The Structure of Politics at the Accession of George III,* a meticulously learned and well-written work, influenced a number of historians to reinterpret English history of the eighteenth century along the lines set down by Sir Lewis. Namier has also been a breaker of tradition in the field of nineteenth and twentieth century diplomatic history, and his 1944 lecture before the British Academy, *1848: The Revolution of the Intellectuals,* electrified the world of scholarship by the stress he laid on nationalism rather than liberalism as the motivating force of the German revolutionaries. The selection given below presents the essential views of Namier in regard to the revolutions of 1848, but in somewhat less vitriolic terms.

T HE MEN of 1848, victorious in Paris, Vienna, and Berlin, stood amazed at their own success and moderation. A revolution had swept over Europe, wider than any before it, but eminently humane in its principles and practice. It had its dead but no victims; it made refugees but no political prisoners. Louis-Philippe crossed the Channel — not the first French ruler nor the last to take to that route. The other sovereigns remained, shaken but not overthrown. Metternich, Guizot, and the Prince of Prussia (the later William I) one by one arrived in London: exponents of three systems, disparate in nature and aims, but seemingly obliterated by the same storm. The strongholds of reaction had fallen, rubble had to be carted away, new structures were to arise; there was a great void, filled by sun and air; and over it brooded a singularly enlightened *Zeitgeist.* Men dreamed dreams and saw visions, and anything the spirit could conceive seemed attainable in that year of unlimited possibilities. Next year the light and airy visions had faded, and it was as if they had never been.

A gale blows down whatever it encounters, and does not distinguish. Revolutions are anonymous, undenominational, and inarticulate. If there is an inherent program, as in agrarian revolutions, it is of a most primitive character. The elemental forces of a mass movement can be made to do the work of men whose quest is alien to them. Most revolutions are filched or deflected: groups or parties with elaborate programs — panaceas or nostrums — try to stamp them with their own ideology and, if successful, claim to be their spokesmen or even their makers. But revolutions are not made; they occur. Discontent with government there always is; still, even when grievous and well founded, it seldom engenders revolution till the moral bases of government have rotted away: which are the feeling of community between the masses and their rulers, and in the rulers a consciousness of their right and capacity to rule. Revolutions are usually preceded by periods of high intellectual achievement and travail, of critical analysis and doubt, of unrest among the educated classes, and of guilt-consciousness in the rulers: so it was in France in 1789, in Europe in 1848, and in Russia in 1917. If such corrosion of the moral and mental bases of government coincides with a period of social upheaval, and the conviction spreads, even to the rulers themselves, that the ramshackle building cannot last, government disintegrates and revolution ensues. Revolutions, as distinct from mere revolts, usually start at the centre of government, in the capital; but the nature of the actual outbreak and its purpose almost invariably escape analysis. What aim did the labouring poor of Paris pursue in the Great Revolution, and what did they attain? What was it that made them fight in July 1830, or in February 1848? And what would they have done had they been successful in the June Days or in the Paris Commune? Agrarian movements are far more articulate in form and aim, and therefore, if extensive and determined, are usually successful. The village is a living organism and its communal consciousness transcends other loyalties; and the peasants' demand to be relieved of dues, or to be given the land of the nobles and the Church, can be met or enforced overnight. The weakness of agrarian movements usually is in that they break out sporadically, and therefore can be suppressed. But if linked with a rising in the urban centres and with self-doubt in the upper classes, if fanned by generalizing factors, such as *la grande peur* in 1789 or the effect of war in 1917, they become overpowering; and then urban groups or parties graft on to them their own programs.

The revolution of 1848 followed on a period of intellectual efflorescence such as Europe has never known before or since; it supervened at a time when the Governments themselves came to feel unequal to the new circumstances and problems; in a period of financial crisis and economic distress, but of disjointed, or even contradictory, social movements. A numerous urban proletariat gathered in the rapidly growing capitals; the independent artisans were fighting a long-drawn losing battle against modern industry; the factory workers started their struggle for a human existence; while the incidence of the agrarian problem was uneven and varied. In France it had been solved by the Great Revolution; in Germany it was confined to several large areas; in the Habsburg Monarchy it was general and acute: there the peasants were determined to sweep away the surviving feudal burdens and jurisdictions. Before the first gusts of the revolutionary storm the Governments collapsed without offering serious resistance; there was a paralysis of will and a consciousness of defeat almost before the fight was joined. But there was no uniform or unified social-revolutionary force to continue the struggle; and the educated middle classes, the successors or new partners of the princes, from an exaggerated fear of the Reds quickly turned counter-revolutionary, though they still counted on preserving the conquests of the initial victory which they had appropriated. The peasants were bought off by timely and extensive concessions; the proletariat was defeated in Paris in the June Days, in Vienna in October, while in Berlin (as in 1933) it succumbed without fighting. In France, where 1789 had done most of the work which still awaited accomplishment elsewhere, 1848 followed a path apart; in the rest of Europe the conflict was between the principle of dynastic property in countries and that of national sovereignty: from which devolved the problems of self-government and self-determination, of constitutional rights and of national union and independence.

The year 1830 brought a reaction against ingenious solutions which the Congress of Vienna had devised for France, Belgium, and Poland; outside France, 1848 was largely an endeavour to find solutions where the Congress had not seriously attempted any. The movement of 1848 was European, yet consciously French in origin. In 1847 Karl Mathy, a Baden bookseller and publisher, had planned a pamphlet putting forward the demands of the German people, to be distributed broadcast on the death of Louis-Philippe: for this was expected to set the European revolution going. "Our revolutions, like our fashions, we were wont to receive from Paris," wrote in 1849 his partner, F. D. Bassermann, a leader of the moderate liberals in the Frankfurt Parliament. The European revolution, when it came, operated within the area of Napoleon's work and influence; for he had sapped inherited forms and loyalties, regrouped territories, established modern administrations, and familiarized tens of millions of men with change in political and social conditions – and new ideas are not nearly as potent as broken habits. When Napoleon was overthrown there had to be restoration. Even had the monarchs and ministers assembled in Vienna wished to reconstruct Europe on a rational basis, how could they by agreement have squared Austrian and Prussian aims and claims in Germany, solved the problem of the Papal State in Italy, or resettled the Habsburg Monarchy on any but dynastic foundations? The failures of 1848 go far to justify 1815. Incapable of devising, men are forced back to the *status quo ante;* and with the pristine facts return ideas in which men no longer wholly believe: in every restoration there is an element of make-believe. The Vienna Congress reaffirmed the idea of indefeasible monarchical rights – and over wide areas failed to restore the previous rulers. And while, for instance, in *Alt-Preussen* and *Alt-Bayern* the countryside was in 1848 *stockpreussisch* and *bayuvarisch,* and therefore hardly affected by revolution, the Roman Catholic Rhineland felt little allegiance to the Hohenzollern, or Protestant Franconia to the Wittelsbach. Nor were the proprietary and quasi-contractual rights attributed to dynasties or Estates compatible with the new social and economic conditions: for those ideas were

connected with the land; they were alien to the intelligentsia (including the bureaucracy which supplied a remarkable percentage of members to the Parliaments of 1848) and to the modern cities. With them conceptions of the neo-horde replace those of rooted populations. In 1848 a considerable advance was made towards the State untrammelled by contract and custom; and a non-territorial, linguistic nationality asserted its sway. The privileged orders entered into partnership with the educated middle classes, accepting their intellectual lead. As early as 12 December 1847 the Prince Consort advised the King of Prussia to meet the coming onslaught by attaching "the well-to-do and intelligent sections of the population – that is, the real people (*das eigentliche Volk*)" to the Government by a share in the administration of the country.

Guizot and Metternich had voluntarily left their countries. Prince William had to be persuaded, nay, made to leave in order to put an end to rumours that he was about to march on Berlin. They quitted, and he did not – and all three proved right; their systems were dead, his was to be the foremost beneficiary of 1848. There was philosophic elevation and spiritual pride in the fallen Ministers, while the Prince was single-minded and *borné* [narrow]. "Je ne connais guère l'embarras et je ne crains pas la responsabilité [I hardly ever recognize difficulties, and I do not fear responsibility]," was Guizot's dictum. "L'erreur ne s'est jamais approché de mon esprit [Mistakes have never entered my mind]," said Metternich with a faint smile when in March 1848 he met Guizot on the steps of the British Museum. But Metternich, on the night of his fall, had replied to his wife: "Oui, ma chère, nous sommes morts [Yes, my dear, we are dead]" – and never again did he try to force his way among the living. Nor did Guizot: in France, he wrote, in great crises the vanquished *deviennent des morts* [become the dead]. Neither was quite of the country he had governed. Metternich, a Rhinelander, had first come to Vienna at the age of twenty-one: the exponent of a non-national ideal, he tried to uphold the Habsburg Monarchy, that dynastic creation *par excellence,* by tying all Europe to the principle which alone could secure Austria's survival. Internal reform he never seriously contemplated: he apprehended its hopelessness — "je passe ma vie à étayer un édifice vermoulu [I spend my life in propping up a worm-eaten structure]." When asked by Guizot to explain how it was that revolution had spread to Austria governed by him, he replied: "J'ai quelquefois gouverné l'Europe, l'Autriche jamais [I have sometimes ruled Europe, but never Austria]." Guizot, on the other hand, was a Protestant attracted by British institutions and ideas, and self-nutured on them, who tried to establish constitutional monarchy in France. Under Louis-Philippe France had enjoyed what the rest of the Continent aspired to in 1848: a Parliamentary régime, equality before the law, civic freedoms. And what Guizot's *toryisme bourgeois* tried to cultivate in France were the civic virtues of Victorian England; "l'esprit de famille, le goût du travail régulier, le respect des supériorités, des lois et des traditions, les sollicitudes prévoyantes, les habitudes religieuses . . . [family spirit, the liking for steady work, respect for one's superiors and for laws and traditions, a cautious prudence, religious habits]." For him French history neither stopped nor started in 1789; he wanted to secure the achievements of the Revolution and lay its ghosts. He thought of "ces millions d'existences qui ne font point de bruit mais qui sont la France [those millions of people who do not raise a fuss but who are the real France]." But beyond these were men he combated and feared:

The French Revolution and the Emperor Napoleon I have thrown a certain number of minds, including some of the most distinguished, into a feverish excitement which becomes a moral and, I would almost say, a mental disease. They yearn for events, immense, sudden, and strange; they busy themselves with making and unmaking governments, nations, religions, society, Europe, the world. . . . They are intoxicated with the greatness of their design, and blind to the chances of success. To hear them talk, one might think that they had the elements and ages at their command . . . and that these were the first days of creation or the last days of the world.

And Louis-Philippe would say to Guizot:

You are a thousand times right; it is in the depth of men's minds that the revolutionary spirit must be fought, for it is there that it reigns; *mais pour chasser les démons, il faudrait un prophète* [but there would have to be a prophet if one wanted to chase out the devils].

Le juste milieu [the "middle way" between absolutism and democracy represented by the Liberal Monarchy of Louis-Philippe] was uninspiring, and no compromise, for neither wing accepted it: to the Legitimists the July Monarchy was a "profanation of monarchy," to the Republicans a perversion and usurpation of national sovereignty. Sainte-Beuve wrote in 1861:

The Orleans dynasty were neither a principle, nor a national glory; they were a utility, an expedient; and they were taken for what they were.

And this was his account of the period:

I appreciated the joys of that reign of eighteen years, the facilities it afforded to the mind and for study, for all pacific pursuits, its humanity, the pleasures offered, even to those not possessed of a vote, by the wonderful display of Parliamentary talent and of eloquence from the tribune. . . . Yet it was impossible to view that régime, in its spirit and ensemble, as in any way grand . . . as something of which one could be proud to have been a contemporary. . . .

Guizot himself writes:

It makes the greatness of our nation . . . that purely material and immediate success does not suffice, and that the mind has to be satisfied as much as the interests.

When the revolution started in the streets of Paris even those who valued the July Monarchy as a "utility" would not die for it. As de Tocqueville puts it "the government was not overthrown, it was allowed to fall." It flopped.

The February Revolution had been universally expected, and after it had occurred no one could account for it. Its course was meaningless, or at least unproductive of immediate results. Memories were relived, and the circle of repetition was completed by the Second Republic, the Presidency of Louis-Napoleon, and the Second Empire. Only in the June Days a new reality pierced through the counterfeit displays; the people of Paris, with a tradition and consciousness of power, but without clear aim, took action. In 1848 the French monarchy was consigned to the grave, and with it an element essential to the proper working of the Parliamentary system was lost. Since then France has faced an uneasy choice between a Parliamentary Republic in which President and Prime Minister to some extent duplicate each other, and a system based on an independent Executive which is a cross between the American Presidency and the Napoleonic dictatorship. The principles of equality and national sovereignty, bequeathed by the Great Revolution, found in 1848 their logical fulfilment in universal suffrage and the Republic, two principles not contravened even by a plebiscitarian Empire. While British radicals adhered to the tenets of classical economy and free trade, French thought in 1848 moved toward new social concepts; the organization and protection of labour, "the right to work" (with its concomitant: relief for the unemployed), universal education as a citizen right, a graduated income-tax — most of which were realized in Britain before they were in France. To begin with, the February Revolution was not anti-clerical, still less anti-religious: the revolutionaries were romantics rather than free-thinkers, while the clergy were largely Legitimists. Lammenais and Lacordaire were forerunners of a socially radical Catholicism. It was only

after the June Days that the cleavage between the Church and the radicals reopened, while the big bourgeois drew closer to the Church in a political clericalism. The problem of Church and State was now sharply put, and the battle joined which was to reach its climax fifty years later.

When Metternich fell, aged seventy-five, he was replaced by Kolowrat, aged seventy, and at the Foreign Office by Ficquelmont, aged seventy-one; in May, Pillersdorf, an official aged only sixty-two, became Prime Minister; but on 8 July he was succeeded by Wessenberg, aged seventy-five, who continued the septuagenarian set-up of Austria's "rejuvenation" till after the October rising in Vienna. And when Bach (aged thirty-five) a politician of revolutionary origin, attained office, within a few weeks he turned into a heavy-handed reactionary. The Vienna revolution was indeed a peculiar affair. But any radical handling of the situation was bound to endanger Austria, immediately or ultimately. Joseph II, Schwarzenberg and Bach, and the men of 1906–14, were exponents of sharp, centralizing authoritarian systems; Maria Theresa, Metternich, and Francis Joseph in his later years temporized; *immer fortwurschteln* ("always muddle along") was the precept of the Emperor's most accordant Premier, Count Taaffe. Where historic survival is both *raison d'être* and aim, logical conceptions are a deadly poison. And Austria survived because of the inherent impossibilities and contradictions of the situation. Metternich knew it, but preferred to bedeck the dismal truth with philosophical dissertations.

The pattern of Austria's existence becomes patent in 1848, though it takes time before it is discerned and the consequences are drawn. There were four dominant nationalities within the Habsburg Monarchy whose upper and middle classes covered also the territories of the subject races: Germans, Italians, Magyars, and Poles, versus Czechs, Slovaks, Yugoslavs, Ruthenes, and Rumans. The four master races demanded a united Germany, a united Italy, an independent Hungary, and a reunited Poland, including between them all the territories of the subject races inhabiting the Monarchy. Their programs carried to their logical conclusion implied the complete disruption of the Austrian Empire, and were therefore opposed by the dynasty, and by those among the Austrian Germans who were more Austrian than German. The subject races, too, desired national unity and independence, but they preferred the rule of the non-national Habsburgs to that of the master races. Some of their leaders, especially among the Czechs, went the length of developing a program of "Austro-Slavism" — of an Austria reconstructed on a Slav basis. But this was a phantasm: for it offered no possible basis for the existence and survival of the Habsburg Monarchy. In the long run the dynasty had to take for partners nationalities which shared their proprietary interests in their territories, as did the Germans, Magyars, and Poles, and which, therefore, were prepared to defend every square mile. But the Germans, inside and outside Austria, would only accept her continued existence in lieu of complete national unity if the German predominance within Austria was maintained and reinforced by a German alliance, which in turn the Habsburgs themselves required to safeguard their dominions; and the Magyars and Poles would only accept it provided it did not touch, and indeed safeguarded, their dominion over Hungary and Galicia. Socially also the German-Magyar-Polish basis best suited the Habsburgs: an ancient dynasty cannot permanently ally itself to peasants against their masters. In 1848–9 the peasant nations supported the dynasty; in 1867 they were abandoned by it to the dominant races. In 1866–7 the German, Italian, and Magyar programs of 1848 were realized in modified forms, and the Polish, in so far as this was possible within the framework of the Habsburg Monarchy alone. In 1918–19 came the time for the subject races of the German and Magyar spheres, and for the Poles; in 1939–45, for the Yugoslavs and Ruthenes in the Italian and Polish spheres. Every idea put forward by the nationalities of the Habsburg Monarchy in 1848 was realized at some juncture, in one form or another. And perhaps even Austro-Slavism will ultimately find its realization in a Danubian Union under Slav ægis.

With 1848 starts the German bid for power, for European predominance, for world dominion: the national movement was the common denominator of the German revolution in 1848, and a mighty Germany, fit to give the law to other nations, its foremost aim. *Einheit, Freiheit, und Macht* ("Unity, Freedom, and Power") was the slogan, with the emphasis on the first and third concepts. "Through power to freedom, this is Germany's predestined path," wrote in April 1848 the outstanding intellectual leader of the Frankfurt assemblies, Professor Dahlmann. Even some of the Republicans were Republicans primarily because they were Nationalists: the existence of thirty-odd dynasties and the rival claims of Habsburgs and Hohenzollerns were the foremost obstacles to German unity, easiest removed by proclaiming a German Republic, one and indivisible. The movement for German unity originated in 1848 in the west, south-west, and in the centre of Germany, in the small States which gave no scope to the German *Wille zur Macht* [Will to power], and in the newly acquired, disaffected provinces of Prussia and Bavaria. But although the aim of the Frankfurt Parliament was a real Pan-Germany, not a Greater Prussia or Great Austria, one of the two German Great Powers had to be the core of the new German Federal State. And here started the difficulties: Austria was the greatest State within the Federation and its traditional "head," but of its 36 million inhabitants less than six were German; while of 16 million in Prussia, 14 were German. Austria obviously could not merge into a German national State, whereas Prussia could — theoretically. It became clear in 1848–9 that a united Greater Germany (*Gross-Deutschland*), comprising the German provinces of Austria, implied the disruption of Austria; otherwise it had to be a Lesser Germany (*Klein-Deutschland*). With an undivided Austria within Germany, the German Confederation could not change into a Federal State; but a Federation of States offered no prospect of real national unity or of power. The Frankfurt Parliament therefore finished by accepting *Klein-Deutschland,* and offered its Crown to the King of Prussia; who refused from respect for Austria and because he could only have accepted the Crown if offered to him by his fellow-sovereigns. Nor would the new Empire as planned at Frankfurt have proved acceptable to the true Prussians: Frankfurt, not Berlin, was to have been its capital, and Prussia was "to merge into Germany" (there was intense jealousy at Frankfurt against the Berlin Parliament, and as a safeguard against Prussian predominance in a *Klein-Deutschland* it was planned to break up Prussia into her eight provinces, each about the size of a German middle-sized State). When in March 1848 Frederick William IV sported the German tricolour and made his troops assume it, the Second Regiment of the Guards replied by a song about "the cry which pierced the faithful hearts: you shall be Prussians no longer, you shall be Germans." When Bismarck showed its text to the Prince of Prussia, tears ran down William's cheeks. But it was his system based on Prussia, her army and administration, which was to be established by the man who showed him the song.

The year 1848 proved in Germany that union could not be achieved through discussion and by agreement; that it could be achieved only by force; that there were not sufficient revolutionary forces in Germany to impose it from below; and that therefore, if it was to be, it had to be imposed by the Prussian army. Again the future was mapped out. There were four programmes in 1848-9. That of *Gross-Oesterreich,* a centralized Germanic Austria, retaining her traditional preponderance in Germany, was realized by Schwarzenberg in 1850, after Olmütz. That of a Greater Prussia was realized in the North German Confederation of 1866, and was extended in 1870-1 to cover the entire territory of the Frankfurt *Klein-Deutschland.* That programme itself, with the capital removed from Berlin, was haltingly attempted under the Weimar Republic; while the other Frankfurt programme of *Gross-Deutschland,* including the German and Czech provinces of Austria, was achieved by Hitler in 1938-9.

In 1800, after some forty years in politics, Lord Shelburne wrote in his memoirs:

It requires experience in government to know the immense distance between planning and executing. All the difficulty is with the last. It requires no small labour to open the eyes of either the public or of individuals, but when that is accomplished, you are not got a third of the way. The real difficulty remains in getting people to apply the principles which they have admitted, and of which they are now so fully convinced. Then springs the mine of private interests and personal animosity. . . . If the Emperor Joseph had been content to sow and not to plant, he would have done more good, and save a great deal of ill.

Most of the men of 1848 lacked political experience, and before a year was out the "trees of liberty" planted by them had withered away. None the less, 1848 remains a seed-plot of history. It crystallized ideas and projected the pattern of things to come; it determined the course of the century which followed. It planned, and its schemes have been realized: but — *non vi si pensa quanto sangue costa* [not if you consider how much blood it costs].

1848 — ONE HUNDRED YEARS AFTER

HANS ROTHFELS

Born and educated in Germany, Hans Rothfels taught at the universities of Berlin and then of Koenigsberg until he was ousted by the Nazis. After a short stay at Oxford, Rothfels came to the United States, lecturing on European history first at Brown University then at the University of Chicago from 1946 until he became emeritus in 1951 and returned to Germany, becoming Professor of Modern European History at the University of Tübingen. Specializing in German history of the nineteenth century, Rothfels takes quite a different view of German developments and of the German national character than do Taylor, Namier, and Ebenstein. His book *The German Opposition to Hitler* (1948) stressed the importance and survival of the liberal or "good" Germany even during Nazi times. In the excerpt from an article on the centenary of 1848 printed here, Rothfels defends the liberal interpretation of the German revolutionaries of 1848.

FAILURE or not, 1848 was a genuine turning-point, and the German notion of *Vormärz* (pre-March) as a distinctive period makes perfectly good sense. In recalling 1848, we recall a divide. In terms of political history this may amount to a truism; even abortive revolutions are bound to have profound effects. The year 1850 no more restored the status of 1847 than 1815 had returned to 1788. Schwarzenberg's dynamic, great-Austrian neoabsolutism, a centralism using liberal means for authoritarian ends, was worlds apart from Metternich's universally conceived system of conservatism, the comparative merits of which have been adequately appraised in our own day. What had been, in the main, an aristocratic society, domestically and internationally, was consolidated or fell apart into more strongly centralized or nationalized fragments — a process which was concomitant with the growing influence of the middle class. However brief the constitutional experiences of 1848–49 had been, in some of the countries concerned they resulted in the strengthening of state unity and the leveling of regional or social inequalities. They left behind universal manhood suffrage as a great legacy of the continental revolution. Forty-eight, as has been said, was the most important year for the whole of Europe's constitutional life. Upon none of the reborn autocratic regimes were the liberal and democratic experiments altogether lost. Neither Otto von Manteuffel's bureaucratic rule of the fifties, coupled as it was with a Prussian liberal constitution, which granted an unequal but general franchise, civil rights, and state-wide representation, nor Karl von Kübeck's and the Forty-eighter Alexander von Bach's Germanizing centralism in Austria and Hungary would have been conceivable before the revolution. And while France had given a new uplift to the republican idea, it also set with Napoleon III the

Reprinted from Hans Rothfels, "1848 — One Hundred Years After," *Journal of Modern History*, XX, 4 (December, 1948), pp. 293–296, 305–313, by permission of the University of Chicago Press. Copyright by the University of Chicago.

pattern for other potentialities of the future. It demonstrated the relationship between a centralized state and an atomized society "à la recherche de l'autorité," i.e., in need of a savior. The upstart who seized upon this role lacked some of the safeguards which hereditary monarchs had evolved. And the example of "authoritarian democracy," of Caesarism based on universal suffrage or on national plebiscites, brought to the fore some of the fateful implications of mass civilization and the danger of moral fatigue. By combining the supreme power with national sovereignty, Napoleon III represented the principle of a new age, as Leopold von Ranke put it in his lectures before Maximilian II of Bavaria in 1854. Or as the pretender, who felt himself to be a "providential" man, had predicted in his *Idées napoléoniennes:* When "the ancient manners" have been destroyed, when in a nation there is no longer an aristocracy or anything "organized" except the army, the social atoms must first be welded together by a "new civil order" before liberty is possible.

Napoleon also proclaimed himself the advocate of the new-fangled principle of nationality. This was part of the "mission of progress" in the interest of which France, again according to the *Idées,* would cast "the sword of Brennus on the side of civilization." It was likewise the potential dynamite directed against the treaties of 1815. Of course, no reaction could stamp out the human feelings which drew people together in what are called "nations." During the revolution this force had proved its strength and, in central Europe at least, had exercised an appeal often superior to that of liberty. Within the following two decades it was more or less successfully applied in the Italian and German unifications. Much as the ways and means (diplomacy and warfare) which were used in 1864–71 differed from those attempted by the men of 1848, it was, in parts at least, their legacy which was carried out, and it was one which bore unmistakably democratic implications. Even Bismarck acknowledged this fact,

prepared if necessary to mobilize the "Acheron" and to "adopt the poor orphan of 1848." He eventually contained the emotional urge (and the unitary principle as well) in the German Empire. Simultaneously, however, the nation-state, that is, a state composed of one nation only with every nation entitled to statehood, came to be applauded, in Western liberal opinion, as the normal form of political life, as a consequence as well as a condition of democracy, and as the vehicle of progress. Citizenship and nationality should be co-extensive, for obviously the question of government ought to be decided by the governed. Thus in 1861 John Stuart Mill, in his *Considerations on representative government,* declared: "It is in general a necessary condition of free institutions that the boundaries of governments should coincide in the main with those of nationalities."

But side by side with this optimistic interpretation, an opposite one could be derived from the experiences of 1848. It became strikingly apparent that the Western practice of equating state with nationality (which was actually patterned after a historic and not an ethnic unit, that is, after the French state-nation) could not be applied to central Europe without dissolving the territorial entities into atoms that would continually struggle with one another. To this extent Metternich's prophecy came true, and it was endorsed by the Austrian poet F. Grillparzer in the ominous words: *Von der Humanität durch die Nationalität zur Bestialität.* With 1848, in fact, a cosmopolitan phase of nationalism passed away. Mazzini's belief in the solidarity of free and democratic nations received a shattering blow as did his Saint-Simonian faith in the coming of a new "organic" age, wherein nationality — an instrument of universal ideas, directed finally toward God — would counteract the atomizing individualism of 1789.

What really happened in 1848 was that, after an initial phase of harmony and liberal enthusiasm, severe clashes occurred not between governments but between peoples.

With some exaggeration, it has been said: "With 1848 starts the Great European War of every nation against its neighbours." At least such a potentiality was inherent in the spread of the principle of nationality within a multinational and ethnically intermixed area. Here democratic rule or national sovereignty was more difficult to reconcile with cultural variety than monarchical government had been. Moreover, with the rise of the so-called "unhistoric," i.e., the merely ethnic, nations — legitimate as was their desire for statehood on the ground of a widely accepted doctrine — a racial rather than a territorial principle was applied. It was the same with Pan-Germanism and Pan-Slavism. In view of these perspectives it is difficult to dismiss as mere insularity the words of an Englishman in 1850: "This barbarous feeling of nationality . . . has become the curse of Europe." In fact, with the appeal to natural and biological forces, materialist and thoroughly heathen concepts entered "national" policies.

Nor was the hope borne out that "free institutions" were promoted by or conditioned upon "the coincidence of boundaries of government with those of nationalities." The elemental force of nationalism had, rather, antiliberal and totalitarian aspects. Thus with the insight of a profoundly religious man and with an Englishman's preference for multicellular life, Lord Acton, the "historian of freedom," raised his voice against the optimistic assumption of John Stuart Mill. In his remarkable essay on "Nationality" (1862) Acton suggested that the "presence of different nations under the same sovereignty" might be as good a thing from the viewpoint of civil liberty as was the independence of the church from the state and that the democratic trend toward uniformity might be as intolerant as that of any autocracy. He spoke of the popular doctrine of unitarism as "insanity" and treated the "principle of nationality" as a retrograde step, ruinous for self-government and for nationality itself. When the rule of democratic self-determination and national fragmentation (Balkanization) was applied

after 1918, a good deal of this prophetic warning came true. And that the elimination of national minorities falls in line with the destruction of civil liberty altogether should be a commonplace since 1933 and 1945.

The first signs pointing in this direction could be seen in 1848. It should be noted in advance, however, that the men of the mid-century were not unaware of this danger. They made at Frankfort, and specifically at Kremsier, considerable effort toward multinational and federal solutions which belongs to the most memorable part of their legacy, a part which has remained unfulfilled. . . .

While all these phenomena are to some extent typical in revolutionary history and were widespread in 1848 throughout the countries involved, they bring the problem of the "German failure" into focus. Within the crucial year, this seems to be more or less accepted as the crucial question: Would not a success of the German revolution, i.e., a timely "Westernization" and democratization of Germany, have helped to turn history in a more promising direction?

In fact, social and international conditions were far from auguring well for such a perspective. But this is not a sufficient answer. Undoubtedly some specific problems of German history are involved in the failure; or as some observers are inclined to state, the failure indicates a characteristic German deficiency. According to this view it is one of the blameworthy things in the general development of this nation that it never carried out a successful revolution. On the basis of either inborn qualities or acquired habits the Germans are simply not made of revolutionary stuff.

It can readily be admitted that the German revolution of 1848 (just like that of 1918) had a certain predilection for "orderly" procedures (incidentally one approved by Americans in 1848) and showed many philistine traits. The Berlin tailor who after the March events painted the Prussian eagle over the door of his shop and wrote underneath, "I can peacefully press under the shadow of thy wings," was no isolated case. And the "freedom to smoke" (even in the *Tiergarten*) may have appeared to many good burghers more important than other achievements of the revolution. It is also undoubtedly true that the German people were still largely parochial, that multiple authority, parceled out as it was among thirty-nine states, and allegiance to small and even tiny entities did not exactly further self-reliance. Even the popular upheavals themselves sometimes resulted in what has been called *gemütliche* anarchy; they were not free of naïve and melodramatic elements which combined strangely with shocking outrages committed by both sides.

On the other hand, it would be unjust to minimize the courage and resoluteness displayed in the actual fighting. The Frenchman Adolphe Circourt, who witnessed the engagements in Paris as well as in Berlin, found that the men of March 18 fought more fiercely than the Parisians had done on February 24. But quite apart from some biases which have clouded these facts (in German as well as in non-German books), there seems to exist, behind the condemnation of German "legalism" and "loyalism," a certain dogmatic assumption which is popular in French and American rather than in English thought and which holds that revolution is good per se. One can easily understand the background of this tradition and the preference for a manifestation of manliness and of an unconditional love of freedom. It was strikingly displayed, for example, in liberal sympathies for the heroic figure of Louis Kossuth, though he was fighting for feudal privileges and against the rights of oppressed nationalities struggling under the Magyar yoke. At any rate, the historian cannot overlook the fact that revolutions are conducive to evil as well as to good and that there are differences between those which may more aptly be called "wars of liberation" and those in which classes or ideologies fight, or try to eliminate, one another in the fashion of religious wars. Moreover, with recent as well as with present experiences in mind, one may wonder whether the somewhat abstract and platonic sympathy with revolutions as such is still so strong in the Western world. Now that the specter of a threat to the traditional way of life and a potential split within national societies has come uncomfortably close, it is perhaps easier to render justice to the men of 1848 and to their sense of crisis.

This is not meant to be an apology for the social shortsightedness which many German liberals of 1848 showed or for their bourgeois instincts. They wore the blinkers of their own time. But in principle history has confirmed their view that the deification of the masses is no sounder political tenet than the deification of the state and that liberty can be threatened from two sides. Certainly, a man of the moral stature of the historian F. C. Dahlmann who in his previous career had given sufficient evidence of civil courage, could claim with good conscience that it was strength rather than weakness to be moderate and not to advocate an abstract ideal of national unity and freedom, which involved the elimination of all dynasties and required other concessions to popular emotions. He spoke of a "noble resistance" to the temptation of power.

But there are the voices of those who doubt the genuineness of such convictions. To them Frankfort stands as a "byword for unreality and phrasemongering"; in their view the majority, i.e., the deputies of the moderate groups, thought that "by talking about human liberty they could conceal their shameful weakness." In fact, it is believed, they sacrificed all principles of freedom and a real social reform to their "dreams of world conquest" and to their national aggressiveness. In sum they proved that they were true representatives of a "destructive people" (Taylor) whose history finds nothing but its natural climax in Hitler.

While the more obvious points of excess and the propaganda slogans in this interpretation can be left aside, the historian, nonetheless, is faced with the striking fact that judgment of the German Forty-eighters and of Frankfort in some respects has gone the full circle. The attitude of contempt and disparagement which Marx and Engels had taken toward the typically liberal trends of the revolution was followed by a sort of lukewarm appraisal in the period of Bismarck (an appraisal tempered by *Realpolitik*). Then evaluation extended to the democratic trends; it became more emphatic particularly after 1918; and in the German celebrations of the centenary, however little there was to celebrate actually, serious efforts have been made to salvage and revive the positive and idealistic elements in the tradition of 1848. At the same time, however, not only has the Marxist view regained credit (even among people who would shudder at the idea of this ancestry), but this has been accompanied by a debunking tendency, by a neorealism, a "surrealism," which tries to discover the "dreams" and the subconscious mentality underlying a surface idealism and which consequently distorts many historic features. This interpretation concentrates on the nationalist aspects of 1848 and of the German revolution in particular.

It is to these specific issues which have been touched only slightly so far and which, in some ways, are closely related to the crisis of our day that attention must finally turn.

As stated before, the social as well as the national issues of 1848 cut fatefully across the liberal problems. While the first intersection had great influence upon French events and affected to a lesser degree those in central Europe, the second complicated the revolution immeasurably among those peoples who had not yet achieved national unity. This can be borne out in a double sense. Not only is it true that the national issue was likely to overshadow the two others, but at the same time it was exposed to grave difficulties and inner inconsistencies which derived from the territorial and ethnic structure of central Europe, from its non-conformity with Western patterns.

This does not seem to apply to the Italian revolution, because in its case liberal and national demands were mainly directed against foreign rulers and were led, or supported, by one native dynasty only. Thus far liberalism and nationalism harmonized with each other. It would also appear that the existence of comparatively clear-cut geographical and linguistic frontiers favored the idea of a "nation one and indivisible." Yet the cry *fino al Brennero* which the Italian partisans raised in the southern Tirol (though theoretical for the time being) was no less contradictory to the national principle (rather more so, in fact) than was, for example, the German insistence upon including the fortress of Posen in the Reich and was motivated by the same strategic considerations. Also, the demand for Trieste and Istria was only partly based on ethnographic ground just as was the German demand for the whole of Schleswig. Moreover, even in the Italian-speaking districts of the southern Tirol difficulties were encountered. The town of Rovereto and a peasant petition with more than a thousand signatures protested against the separatist aims. As in many other places in central Europe, linguistic, i.e., objective, criteria proved to be by no means identical with the subjective criteria of nationality. For economic and historical reasons the idea of the territorial unity of the northern and southern Tirol reasserted itself. However, it was not these difficulties at the periphery but military defeat, rather, that caused the failure of the Italian revolution of 1848.

The German situation, on the other hand, showed the full complexity involved in effectuating the nation-state idea. For one thing, and in contrast to Italy, the separate German political units, however artificial in origin many of them were, had, in the main, a firmer basis in dynastic allegiance; none was ruled by a foreigner, though the two predominant states were German and European at the same time. They belonged with only parts of their territory to the Confederation of 1815, and in the Austrian case this part, of course, was not exclusively

German. Political multiplicity and cultural variety thus opposed from the outset any strictly unitary solution, whether monarchical or republican.

In fact, even before military and bureaucratic reaction took hold of the major German states and sustained them against the claims of a national parliament, the revolution itself had strengthened the individual entities. This effect had previously been experienced to some extent in the newly created and enlarged kingdoms in southern Germany when they entered constitutional life. It became strikingly apparent in 1848 in the Prussian case. While a liberal constitution in Prussia would make this state more popular and its leadership more attractive, it would also add to the difficulty of absorbing Prussia into Germany. For this reason it was a very plausible demand of some southwestern liberals that Prussia should abstain from completing its state unity with a rival parliament based on universal manhood suffrage. Advocates of Prussian leadership though these Frankfort deputies were, they wanted, of course, a conquest of Prussia by Germany, not one of Germany by Prussia. But there was a basic paradox in their practically falling in line with the old conservative thesis that Prussia, a "federative" state, should have a representation based on provincial estates only. A split opened between Prussian and German liberals when the Constituent Assembly in Berlin actually convened. The allegedly anti-Prussian liberals from the Rhineland were as much against dissolving a state, the leadership of which they now held, as the Prussian Social Democrats were to be after 1918. Moreover, the Berlin parliament was more leftist in its composition than that of Frankfort; it was by no means inclined to submit to the would-be national sovereign or to accept the prior claim of Frankfort legislation over Berlin legislation.

The dilemma in which the German liberals found themselves came into the open when the failure of the second Vienna revolution in October brought the constitutional crisis to Prussia. They could desire neither the triumph of the reaction nor that of the Berlin assembly. In consequence they fell between the stools. The outcome of the crisis was that the new Prussian government dissolved the constituent parliament in December but at the same time decreed a surprisingly liberal constitution which set the seal upon Prussian state unity. In spite of all conflicts between the royal government and the Berlin parliament, the coherence of a specific state-nation had won rather than lost through the revolutionary movement. However personal the motives of Frederick William IV were when he rejected the Frankfort crown, there is no doubt that the Prussian people were no more willing to be "mediatized" for the sake of German unity than was the king. No serious upheaval occurred in Prussia in favor of the Frankfort constitution and its offer of a Hohenzollern *Erbkaisertum* such as occurred in some of the smaller states.

Parallel effects resulted from the liberal and democratic experiences in the Austrian part of the German Confederation and from the existence, in particular, of a central parliament in Vienna. Moreover, Schwarzenberg's dissolution of the Austrian reichstag in March 1849 and the promise of a liberal constitution to be given by the crown were replicas of the Prussian events of December 1848. Other important factors, however, which have more directly to do with the national questions also had a share in strengthening the reassertion of the Habsburg monarchy.

Admittedly, it was the reviving vitality of the two major states, the unwillingness of the one to be dissolved into provinces and of the other to be split into two parts, which formed one great difficulty in the path of German unification. Another problem arose from the necessity of choosing between the two states, and this led to the *kleindeutsch-grossdeutsch* division. It has often been regretted that the Frankfort parliament did not force these issues while moral superiority was still on its side, when governments were shaken and conditions were malleable, but rather devoted most of the summer and autumn to working out a bill of fundamental rights (*Grundrechte*) — to the "interior decoration" of a house not yet existing. Such a procedure seems to be particular evidence of the lacking sense of reality or the "academic" character of the Frankfort assembly. About this character, indeed, there is no doubt. With three-quarters of the deputies former university students, with fifty-seven schoolmasters and forty-nine university professors or lecturers in attendance, the first German reichstag of modern times was certainly the most highly educated parliament in constitutional history. And before criticizing its "theoretical" attitude, historical justice requires the acknowledgment of the intellectual level of the debates, the ethical standards displayed, and the absence of lobbying pressure groups or merely materialist interests. Perhaps it is a prejudice of our own day that ideas are no reality, and the centenary properly reminds us of certain fallacies into which such a belief has led.

But other qualifications have to be added to this appraisal. After all, the Frankfort "professors" were obviously not so utopian or doctrinaire as an old convention has it. One might rather criticize (as some have done) their opportunism — their willingness to compromise and to take realities too much or too early into account. This was certainly one of the reasons why they side-stepped the most critical national issue. Yet it was not the only one. The "fundamental rights" were much more than an academic pastime or an attempt to cover "shameful weakness" with high-sounding phrases; they were a basic concern of liberals. And one cannot very well criticize the primary devotion to the principles of freedom as a policy which evaded the most urgent problem of national unification and at the same time, or in a general way, blame the Frankfort assembly for sacrificing liberalism in favor of nationalist aims. Moreover, those who are so eager today to debunk the idealism of a parliament, "mis-takenly called noble" (Namier), and who see nothing but phrasemongering in its more principled professions are apparently in danger of undermining their own standards, i.e., of sharing the contempt for "liberal impotence" so common to Nazi and Soviet writers.

In view of the recent double attack upon basic values of the Western world and in view of the fundamental importance which the safeguarding of "human dignity" has won, even in countries where bourgeois society has practically disappeared, it may be very worth while to commemorate the efforts (however theoretical in some aspects) which the men of the Church of St. Paul devoted to the substance of the liberal ideal. They followed the American and the French examples, though with significant deviations. The fundamental rights had less of a general and propagandist character; they were less universally conceived than the "rights of men and citizens." Some of the main authors (Jacob Grimm and, in particular, Georg Beseler) were heads of the historical school which opposed the natural-law doctrine. Moreover, all emphasis was placed on personal freedom — spiritual, intellectual, political, and civil. At Frankfort one liked to speak of a "German Habeas Corpus Act," and the very notion of the *Rechtsstaat* was coined in the debates.

Egalitarian and democratic demands met with less sympathy. While equality before the law and the removal of all privileges were stressed, the plan to abolish noble status, titles, and orders fell through. It was the companion of the Freiherr vom Stein, the old Ernst Moritz Arndt, who in professing himself a republican spoke nonetheless against transforming social and (political) variety into uniformity. There was no intention of completely leveling historic differentiations. And Grimm expressly stated that men are not "born equal." One may add that the weakest part of the fundamental rights was the one which dealt with economic and social matters. It breathed liberalism pure and simple, i.e., full confidence in the harmonious effects of competition and in the soundness of the law of supply and demand. In accordance with this creed the right of property and its inviolability found recognition without any ethical obligations attached. A progressive step was that, together with freedom of enterprise, the freedom of association was proclaimed. The majority, however, rejected not only the famous "right to work" which was compromised by the June days in Paris but also the numerous motions and the many petitions from outside which urged what a democratic deputy called the "right not to starve" or the "freedom of existence" for artisans and workers.

These limits, which were the limitations of classical liberalism, have to be stated; and it is also obvious that with the defeat of the Frankfort constitution and with the renunciation of the fundamental rights by the renewed diet of the German Confederation the whole program remained theoretical. It would be wrong, however, to call it impractical and altogether lacking in results. The Frankfort principles were incorporated in the constitutions of some of the individual states (in part this applies also to Prussia) and came to life in the juristic codes and in the economic legislation of the German reich after 1866 and 1870. It is well known that they were revived more expressly in the Weimar constitution and in those of the present western German *Länder*.

While the fundamental rights were still under debate (they were promulgated in December), the critical national problem came eventually to the fore with the Vienna events in October. The victory of the Habsburg dynasty over the second revolution, won to some degree with the help of South Slavic forces (Jellačić), weakened the *grossdeutsche* front by making it unlikely that the Habsburg empire was going to be transformed into a personal union, which process alone would enable the Austrian Germans to join the Reich. It is not to be described here how the *kleindeutsche* solution progressed from October to January and even-

tually to the election of Frederick William IV in March 1849. The point of interest for the present discussion is, rather, that it meant a retreat (even in the form of H. von Gagern's program of a subsequent alliance between *Kleindeutschland* and Austria) and was certainly far from "Pan-Germanism." It would appear that the "professorial lambs" who in the early months of the "glorious" revolution "caught rabies" when "bitten by the Pan-German dog" made at least a surprisingly quick recovery. In fact, some of them had favored *Kleindeutschland* from the beginning. Nor is it easy to maintain that they were ready to sacrifice democratic reform for the sake of national aggressiveness. The reverse, rather, was true in this phase. In order to rescue *Kleindeutschland* and to win a majority for the election of Frederick William IV, the liberals had to grant concessions to the Left (full extension of universal suffrage and a suspensive veto) — concessions in a unitary and democratic direction which were bound to make the "revolutionary" crown even more unpalatable to the Prussian king.

But the Prusso-German and the Austro-German problems were not the only stumbling blocks in the way of unification. As indicated before, the very principle of nationality, while spreading from the west, revealed its true "demony" when applied to historic central Europe. In view of these broader aspects it is not unfair to speak of an aggressive and expansionist spirit among the German (and other) Forty-eighters. And except for some reservations, one can agree with Namier's statement that the conservatives (and not the social revolutionaries) "preserved peace in Europe" and that German nationalism in particular derived "from the much belauded Frankfort parliament rather than from Bismarck and Prussianism." In fact, this is a basic insight into the problems of the later nineteenth century as well as into present issues, and one can only regret that it has won credit among Anglo-Saxon writers so belatedly. But qualifications must be added. And to call the German liberals "forerunners" of Hitler

(Namier) seems to be as questionable as the indiscriminate use of "Pan-Germanism," *Drang nach Osten,* "prelude to Brest Litovsk," and so on.

Space does not permit a closer examination of the problems and difficulties connected with the national concepts and attitudes of the German revolution. These problems concern the frontiers which were envisaged for the new reich. Only a few facts may be stressed. On the one hand, the Frankfort parliament in principle kept within the boundaries of the German Confederation, which after all were internationally guaranteed. On such a territorial basis, of course, no purely national state, no nation-state could be built. But the prevailing concept was by no means an ethnic and even less a Pan-Germanic one; it was rather that of political "nationality," taken in the unassuming meaning of the French or English vocabulary, that is, as an equivalent of "citizenship." Thus the democratic deputy W. Jordan in one of his less well-known speeches said in Frankfort: "Nationality is no longer limited by descent and language, but is simply determined by the political organism, the state." He was seconded by the liberal G. Beseler, who characterized it as a great disadvantage that heretofore in Germany one had regarded "state" and "nationality" as distinct. "Now," he continued, "citizenship and nationality are coinciding just as in Belgium and France." He hailed this as "progress."

The acceptance of such a Western pattern had in some respects definite consequences of restraint. No claims were raised, on the basis of language and descent, with regard to Alsace, to say nothing of the Flemings or of the Germans in Switzerland. To that extent Frankfort respected state frontiers and subjective nationality. Nor was the proposal sustained to extend an invitation to the Germans in the Baltic Provinces. There had been some Pan-German interest in this direction, particularly among south German liberals. But Frankfort clearly realized that the new reich could not be based on an ethnic principle without calling for expansion on almost all sides and without leading to a demolition of all historic structures. No Hitlerian interest was shown in the "racial comrades abroad" save for a merely cultural one (e.g., in Transylvania). There was desire for power and national greatness but no "dream of world conquest." . . .

THE CENTENARY OF 1848 IN GERMANY AND AUSTRIA

G. P. GOOCH

George Peabody Gooch is the dean of living English historians. He has written on a wide variety of subjects, including English political thought in the early modern period, nineteenth century historiography, German history of the eighteenth and nineteenth centuries, and, most importantly, the diplomatic relations of the powers in the period preceding the First World War. The selection given below is a lecture given at the London School of Economics and Political Science in February of 1948 to commemorate the centennial of 1848; in it he assesses the contradictory interpretations of the "Year of Revolutions" in Germany and Austria, striking a balance sheet between what he considers its accomplishments and its failures.

THE OUTSTANDING political achievement of the German people in the nineteenth century was the creation of a nation-state, and the Year of Revolutions was a milestone on the road. It is the story of a courageous experiment, of a bitter disappointment, of high-minded patriots confronted by a superhuman task. Yet it was not wholly a failure, for it formulated lofty ideals and bequeathed inspiring memories. Few historic conflicts on a wide front are won at the first attack.

The battle of Waterloo ended a struggle which had lasted for twenty-three years, and inaugurated an era in which, at any rate during the earlier phases, the predominant desire was for a quiet life, a breathing space, the chance to heal the gaping wounds of war. The thirty-three years of peace were the longest period without a major military struggle which Europe has enjoyed for centuries. It has been called by many names — the age of reaction, the age of stagnation, the age of Metternich — but it is best described as the Restoration Era.

During the first half a concerted endeavour was made by the Holy Alliance and the Concert of Europe to undo or — if that should prove impossible — to limit the work of the French Revolution. In several countries — Italy, Spain, Germany and Austria — the counter-revolution was generally successful; in England and France, happily for their citizens, it failed.

Germany after 1815, to use Metternich's contemptuous phrase about Italy, was merely a geographical expression. The German Confederation established by the Treaty of Vienna was a considerable improvement on the Holy Roman Empire, which after a thousand years had vanished like a ghost at a touch of Napoleon's spear; but it was a radically imperfect embodiment of the hopes of national integration generated by the War of Liberation. The Diet, composed of nominated representatives of the members of the Bund, sat at Frankfurt in permanent session, but that was the only organ. It had no head, no Ministers, no capital, no army, no repre-

From G. P. Gooch, "The Centenary of 1848 in Germany and Austria," *Contemporary Review*, Vol. 173 (April, 1948), pp. 220–226. By permission of the *Contemporary Review*.

sentatives abroad; it was merely a loose grouping of sovereign states sundered by memories of bloody strife and paralysed by the rivalry between Austria and Prussia. Its story down to 1847 has been told by Treitschke in the most brilliant work ever written on modern Germany, and "the Bismarck of the Chair" exhausts his copious vocabulary of invective on its sorry impotence. The heavy hand of Metternich lay upon it. The Carlsbad Decrees embodied the static philosophy of a man who regarded the French Revolution as an odious interruption of the traditional life of feudal Europe and the *Burschenschaften* (students' unions) as nests of conspirators to be rooted out.

In the Hapsburg Empire the hands of the clock moved slowly under the paternal sway of the Emperor Francis, and under Ferdinand, his half-witted son, they almost stood still. Authority was shared in an uneasy partnership between Metternich, who controlled foreign affairs, and Kolowrat, who looked after the finances and decided the main issues in the domestic sphere. After the reforming era of Maria Theresa and her gifted sons Joseph and Leopold, and after the excursions and alarms of the Great French War, it was a time of outward tranquillity if not of inner repose. Metternich knew that he was simply propping up a tottering edifice, and lamented that his lot was cast in such a dull and exhausted generation. All that can be said for him and his system has been advanced in Srbik's monumental biography and in Mr. Algernon Cecil's thoughtful study. The most balanced appraisement is to be found in Professor Woodward's *Three Essays on European Conservatism*. His best quality was his conception of Europe as an organic whole.

In the enthusiasm of the War of Liberation, and with the inspiring memory of the Stein-Hardenberg reforms fresh in mind, Frederick William III had promised his people a constitutional advance. The promise was never fulfilled. He only permitted the creation of Diets in the eight provinces

which formed the Prussian State; but there was no tie connecting them and no prospect of a constitution. In Berlin as in Vienna stagnation was the order of the day. The fashionable philosopher was Hegel, who proclaimed in majestic tones the omnipotence of the State, and was accused by irreverent critics of mistaking the kingdom of Prussia for the Kingdom of Heaven. Yet the Hohenzollerns did more for their citizens than the Hapsburgs. Prussia took the lead in the construction of the Zollverein, which needed a generation to expand over the larger part of Germany and to which Austria never adhered. And there were other encouraging factors to record. The Prussian bureaucracy was perhaps the best in Europe. Justice was fairly administered, the Press was free, and the universities hummed with the fruitful activities which rapidly won for German scholarship its place at the top of the list.

The French Revolution of 1830, which substituted the Bourgeois Monarchy of Louis Philippe for the Bourbon intransigence of Charles X, produced scarcely more than a ripple across the Rhine. The eccentric Duke of Brunswick was chased away, but Prussia was unaffected. The accession of the artistic and scholarly Frederick William IV in 1840 seemed like the coming of spring. But the hopes were short-lived, for the spiritual home of the romantic monarch was in the Middle Ages, and he cherished the idea of the Divine Right of Kings as firmly as James I and Charles I. He was equally convinced that the first place in the German Confederation belonged by right to the House of Hapsburg, and that the Hohenzollerns could and should only play second fiddle. There was, however, a good deal of earnest discussion in court circles about the possibility of constitutional advance, and in the spring of 1847 the members of the eight provincial Diets were summoned to a joint meeting at Berlin. "The United Diet" was a prologue to the more representative assemblies of the following years. Conservative though it was, the majority of its members requested periodical meetings and a share in the control of finance. Neither was granted, and it was dissolved after animated debates, in which Bismarck made his début, when it had sat for two months.

On the eve of 1848 Prussia and Austria, the two major members of the Bund, lagged far behind the South German States, all of which had been granted constitutions soon after the return of peace. Weimar under Karl August had taken the lead, to the disgust of the ageing Goethe, who had no use for democracy. Liberalism was strongest in the Rhineland, where French ideas of equality and the sovereignty of the people had taken root during the twenty years of the occupation. While Right Wing Liberals of the north, with the historian Dahlmann at their head, looked to England as their model, Left-Wingers of the south, led by Rotteck and Welcker, the standard-bearers of Baden radicalism, turned their eyes to Paris. In Hanover a constitution granted after the French Revolution of 1830 was torn up in 1837 by King Ernest Augustus, the detestable uncle of Queen Victoria, and the famous "Göttingen Seven" — Professors at the State University — were dismissed from their chairs as a penalty for their protest. While politically speaking Germany before 1848 was not, like Austria, a land of almost total darkness, there were only fitful gleams of light. Once again, as in the time of the first French Revolution, a vigorous shock from abroad was required to mobilise the liberal forces which had slowly developed during three decades of stifling control.

The earliest rumblings were heard in Italy in January, but it was the eruption in Paris in February 1848 which set half the Continent alight. When France has a cold, remarked Metternich after the revolution of 1830, all Europe sneezes. Since Guizot obstinately declined to extend the franchise beyond the narrow ranks of the prosperous bourgeoisie, Louis Philippe was evicted as easily as Charles X in 1830, and the Second Republic was proclaimed. The repercussion throughout Central Europe

was instantaneous. A demonstration in Vienna on March 12th toppled down the Government; Metternich, like Louis Philippe, escaped to England, and the court fled to Innsbruck. A Constituent Assembly met, and throughout the spring and summer the constitutionalists were in control. Their principal achievement was the abolition of serfdom. The army could have snuffed out the revolt like the flame of a candle, but for the moment it was required to deal with the troubles in Lombardy and Venetia. Moreover, now Metternich and Kolowrat were gone, there was no one in the entourage of the feeble Emperor to seize the reins with a firm hand.

The authority of the Hapsburgs was challenged with equal success in Hungary which, at the opening of 1848, had no desire to break away from the Empire, but which longed for full autonomy. The students in Budapest formed a committee when the news from Paris arrived, and on March 15th they drafted the Twelve Points which became the watchword of the national movement. Their leaders were Petöfi, the poet, soon to die fighting in the war of liberation, and Maurus Jokai, later to earn world-wide renown as the Hungarian Walter Scott. The principal demands were for Parliamentary Government, the abolition of serfdom and feudal privileges, and a free Press. They were carried to Vienna by Kossuth, in whom the national movement found an inspiring chief, and Count Batthyany, who was commissioned to form a Ministry. In this the best men in Hungary, among them Kossuth and Szechenyi, Eötvös and Deak, held posts. Almost overnight the country was transformed from a subordinate province into a modern self-governing community.

A similar spectacle of unresisted emancipation was witnessed at Prague. After two centuries of oppression following the disaster at the battle of the White Mountain in 1620, Czech nationalism was revived in the opening decades of the nineteenth century by a little group of scholars with the illustrious historian Palacky at their head.

Once again their readers and hearers began to feel pride in their history and literature, and when the hour struck in 1848 they were ready to act. In the eventful month of March a mass meeting petitioned Vienna for equal rights for the Czech language in all the Government offices, for a Diet of all the Bohemian lands elected on a wide franchise, and for certain overdue reforms. A meeting of the Estates, empowered to draft a constitution, was promised in April and elected in May. It never met, since a far more comprehensive scheme took shape of a Congress for Slavs from all over Austria and from other lands. The Panslav Congress of Prague, in which Palacky played the leading part, holds the same honoured place in the evolution of Slav nationalism as the Frankfurt Parliament in German annals, but its career was even shorter. When riots broke out in June the capital was bombarded and capitulated to Windischgrätz. Bohemian nationalism was once more submerged though not destroyed. Czechs sat in the Austrian Constituent Assembly at Vienna, but that also was suppressed in the autumn. The absolutist régime was restored, and the work begun by Palacky and the men of 1848 had to wait for a new leader, Thomas Masaryk, half a century later.

In the same week which witnessed the collapse of the old régime in the three Hapsburg capitals the pent-up dissatisfaction of Berlin broke into open revolt. The March Days (March 15th–18th) form a historic landmark, not merely because they ended the Restoration era and buried the doctrine of the Divine Right of Kings, but because they encouraged reformers all over Germany to act. Frederick William IV, well described as all nerves and no muscle, detested bloodshed; and though his troops could have trampled the revolt under their feet, he capitulated at the first challenge. The United Diet was recalled but was quickly superseded by a Constituent Assembly elected by universal male suffrage, and a Liberal Ministry was installed. The distracted King bided his time, with wrath in his heart as he watched the tornado sweeping across Central Europe. The simultaneous revolution in Munich, resulting in the abdication of King Ludwig, was a storm in a teacup, for it was due less to the strength of Liberal convictions than to resentment at the infatuation of the elderly monarch for the foreign dancer, Lola Montez. More serious because more strictly political was a revolt in Baden, by far the most radical member of the Bund.

The supreme achievement of the Year of Revolution in Central Europe was the Frankfurt Parliament, which, like other memorable events, has given rise to contradictory judgments. German Liberals, like the historian Veit Valentin, himself a Frankfurter and author of the most comprehensive survey of the hopes and fears and struggles of 1848, look back to it with admiration and respect. Men of other schools follow Bismarck in contemptuously dismissing it as "the Professors' Parliament." In his recent work, *1848: The Revolution of the Intellectuals,* Professor Namier denies its claim to embody Liberal principles, and labels its spokesmen forerunners of Hitler on the ground that they denied to Czechs, Poles and Danes the rights they claimed for themselves.

Whatever our verdict there is general agreement that it contained many of the most gifted men of the time. Juridically the Bund remained intact, but when the revolutionary blast swept across the Rhine the Diet ceased to meet. Now that Austrian and Prussian reformers had asserted themselves, might not something be done for the German people as a whole? The question was asked and answered by a gathering at Heidelberg of fifty Liberals from the South and West, of whom the moving spirit was Heinrich von Gagern, the standard-bearer of Liberalism in Hesse-Darmstadt. It was decided to invite all members of existing legislatures and a number of selected notables to meet at Frankfurt in order to prepare the way for a Constituent Assembly. The invitation was promptly accepted. The so-called Preliminary Parliament met at

Frankfurt on March 31st, and its five hundred members agreed to summon a National Assembly elected by universal suffrage. A new spirit was revealed when Germany, the land of obedience as Herder called it, witnessed a major political initiative by private citizens without seeking permission from their Hapsburg or Hohenzollern masters.

The Frankfurt Parliament assembled in St. Paul's Church on May 18th. Though "the Professors' Parliament" is far too narrow a title to be accurate, it was above all a gathering of the educated bourgeoisie — professors, schoolmasters, judges, lawyers, civil servants, journalists, with a sprinkling of pastors and priests. A Polish peasant from Silesia was the only representative of the Fourth Estate, for the member states of the Bund were still predominantly agricultural communities. The first step to industrialisation had only just been taken in the construction of a few railways, and the firm of Krupp was in its infancy. The Communist Manifesto was the work of two Germans, Marx and Engels, but it was drafted and published outside Germany. The leading figures of the Frankfurt Parliament were good citizens bent on procuring for their country the privileges of national integration and constitutional government already enjoyed elsewhere. Gagern was the obvious choice for its first president, and among the academic celebrities who adorned its benches were the historians Dahlmann and Gervinus, Jakob Grimm, Droysen, Duncker and Waitz. The appearance of the veteran Arndt at the tribune seemed to link up 1848 with the distant heroic era of the War of Liberation.

The principal task of the Frankfurt Parliament was to draft a constitution which should supersede the anæmic Bund. The discussions, in which Dahlmann, Professor of History at Bonn, took the leading part, continued throughout the year. A Bundesstaat (Federation), it was generally agreed, must take the place of the Staatenbund (Confederation) created in 1815, but it was obviously far more difficult to construct. It was much the same problem which had confronted the Fathers of the American Constitution — to combine the authority of the central organs with reasonable autonomy for the federal units. The final draft provided for two Houses, the Upper Chamber representing the States, the Lower elected by universal male suffrage; the responsibility of Ministers to Parliament; a hereditary Emperor with a suspensive veto; a Supreme Court; and — last, not least — a statement of the fundamental rights (Grundrechte) of the citizen. All German lands were entitled and expected to join the Federation. Pending the establishment of the new system a regent or administrator of the Reich (Reichsverweser) was needed. This responsible post was offered to and accepted by the Archduke John, a younger brother of the Emperor Francis, and uncle of the reigning Emperor Ferdinand. He was reputed the most liberal of the Hapsburgs, and to the end he loyally played his part. Though he appointed a Ministry with Gagern at the head, the new executive possessed no authority whatever, no army, no diplomatic representatives. Indeed, the whole Frankfurt experiment had been rendered possible owing to the temporary preoccupation of Austria and Prussia with internal difficulties. As soon as their armies were again available at the close of 1848 the sword was thrown into the scales, and the structure collapsed like a house of cards.

The counter-revolution in Central Europe started where the revolution itself had begun — in Vienna. When Radetzky had suppressed the rebellion in Lombardy, the authority of the dynasty was forcibly restored in the capital by Windischgrätz after a bloody struggle. The feeble Ferdinand abdicated and was succeeded by his nephew Francis Joseph, a lad of eighteen who was destined to rule over the polyglot empire for sixty-eight years. At his side stood the formidable Prince Schwarzenberg, described by his master long afterwards as the ablest of his many ministers. The revolution was also quickly suppressed in Bohemia and Hungary. In the latter case Russian troops were despatched by the Emperor Nicholas to the aid of the Hapsburgs. When the rebels capitulated at Vilagos in the summer of 1849, there were terrible reprisals. Count Batthyany, the Premier, and seven generals were executed. Kossuth escaped a similar fate by flight to Turkey and later to Italy, and he never saw his country again. The triumph of the counter-revolution in Prussia proved an easier affair. Realising that the revolutionary impetus had spent itself, and urged on by the unofficial Camarilla which guided his faltering steps, Frederick William IV at last determined to restore the authority of the Crown. He appointed Count Brandenburg, an illegitimate son of Frederick William II, as his chief Minister, dissolved the Chamber, and issued a new and narrowly limited constitution. To use his own drastic expression, he swept out the democratic dirt of the year of shame. By the close of 1848 the tide which had run so strongly in the spring and summer had ebbed, and the ancient landmarks reappeared above the flood.

The triumph of dynastic reaction in Austria and Prussia sealed the fate of the Frankfurt Parliament. It was now little more than a debating society, for at any moment it might be dissolved. Since neither Vienna nor Berlin had been consulted about its creation, they did not feel the slightest obligation to preserve its life. Their desire was to restore the Bund which, however little it satisfied German opinion, was good enough for them both. Thus when the Imperial crown was offered to the King of Prussia in the spring of 1849, it was contemptuously refused on the ground that the princes alone had the right to offer such a glittering prize: to the mystical believer in Divine Right its democratic taint was an offence. But there was a further reason. The Hapsburg Emperor, he felt, had a stronger claim, and in any case he lacked the courage to incur his displeasure. He was right to decline the offer, for he regarded Constitutional Monarchy as a con-

tradiction in terms, and he was too honourable a man to sacrifice his convictions. His refusal was the *coup de grâce* to the Frankfurt Parliament, whose members began to melt away. A few endeavoured to carry on the struggle in a Rump Assembly at Stuttgart, but the gas had gone out of the brightly tinted balloon. Finally the Archduke John himself resigned. An attempt was made to save something from the wreck when Radowitz, the most intimate friend and counsellor of Frederick William IV, founded the so-called Prussian Union, which was joined by Saxony, Hanover, and other North German states. Representatives met in Erfurt in March 1850, but the union had a short life, for Schwarzenberg was now firmly in the saddle at Vienna, and was determined to use his power. Saxony and Hanover resigned, the union was dissolved, the Bund was restored, and Austria imposed her will on Prussia by threat of war in the Convention of Olmütz at the close of 1850. The revolution was over. Looking back, we can see that it never had a chance, for the big battalions were on the other side.

Let us attempt a rough balance sheet of 1848–9. In the first place German Liberalism received a blow from which it never recovered, and its ranks were thinned by the flight of some of its bravest champions, among them Carl Schurz, to the New World. Secondly, though the constitutions and institutions of 1848 were quickly swept away, the desire for a nation-state survived in the hearts and minds of millions. Thirdly, the collapse of the Frankfurt Parliament suggested to Bismarck — and not to Prussian statesmen alone — that Austria's veto on the creation of an effective German federation could only be removed by force. For the plan of admitting merely her German provinces was naturally rejected at Vienna, while the inclusion of the Austro-Hungarian Empire as a whole would involve dilution by large blocks of non-German citizens. Though Bismarck scoffed at the Frankfurt Parliament, its failure facilitated his work, and he used parts of its constitutional scheme for the North German Confederation of 1867 and for the Empire in 1871. Yet it is not a record of total failure, for two significant entries are to be found on the credit side. The abolition of serfdom in the realm of the Hapsburgs is a landmark in the history of the fourth estate, and the Prussian Constitution granted by Frederick William IV in 1850 continued to operate till the fall of the Hohenzollerns in 1918. Memories of effort and failure are often the most potent inspiration to new endeavours. The spirit of 1848 seemed to be reincarnate in Friedrich Naumann and the other makers of the Weimar Constitution in 1919. Their work, too, has perished. To-day the chief foes of constitutional and national liberty are no longer Hapsburgs and Hohenzollerns, but men of non-German blood. Yet it is too soon to conclude that the world has heard the last of the ideas and ideals of 1848.

THE REVOLUTION OF THE SPIRIT

PRISCILLA ROBERTSON

Daughter of the late Preserved Smith, one of America's most distinguished historians, Priscilla Smith Robertson made a notable contribution to history in her *Revolutions of 1848*. The book was subtitled "a social history" because she attempted to "show how men lived and felt" rather than to describe constitutions, battles, and rulers. By her brilliant characterizations of events and personalities, Mrs. Robertson succeeded in producing a book which was both scholarly and fascinating. The following selection is the final chapter in the book and gives her reasons why she considers the revolutions a complete failure.

Most of what the men of 1848 fought for was brought about within a quarter of a century, and the men who accomplished it were most of them specific enemies of the 1848 movement. Thiers ushered in a third French Republic, Bismarck united Germany, and Cavour, Italy. Deák won autonomy for Hungary within a dual monarchy; a Russian czar freed the serfs; and the British manufacturing classes moved toward the freedoms of the People's Charter.

That these things could happen showed that the aims of the revolutionists were not dangerous to the structure of society, only their methods. A person who has power may use his power to create changes, yet violently resist having others take power from him so that they could make the same or better changes. In 1848 what neither the governments nor the moderate leaders could brook was popular agitation and popular control. The historian Trevelyan regrets that 1848 could not have seen successful liberal regimes established before the class struggle became acute as it did later in the century. But in a sense the 1848 revolutions turned into class struggles, and failed because they did. In every

country appeared a split between two groups which cooperated at first in the struggle against authority, between the forces typified by Lamartine and those by Louis Blanc, Heinrich von Gagern and Robert Blum, the Reading Club and the Aula in Vienna, between Deák and Kossuth, Cavour and Mazzini. In those countries which, like Hungary and Italy, were struggling against a foreign oppressor, the conflict of nationalities made a screen to hide the conflict of classes. But Deák would not have relished Kossuth's success, nor Cavour Mazzini's.

This is true despite the belief of the leaders of all the parties that the conciliation of classes was the greatest gain that could come from a new government, and despite their hope that by this revolution the class struggle could be avoided. During the generation before 1848 fear of the lower classes was growing, and the men then in power could only bridle the workers with work, as Guizot proposed, or, like Metternich, clamp on a lid which they knew to be temporary. The reformers turned these fears inside out, saying that by kindness the working classes could be won away from the class struggle and given an

From Priscilla Robertson, *Revolutions of 1848: A Social History* (Princeton, N. J., 1952), pp. 412–419. By permission of Princeton University Press.

honored place in society. This doctrine had many intellectual ancestors; in 1848 it was propagated by men like Louis Blanc and Mazzini. Yet this view was not the property of the radical parties alone. Lamartine declared on February 24 that the Second Republic would suspend the frightful misunderstanding that had grown up between classes; Cavour thought that in fusion of classes lay the principal strength of modern society.

When governments with this hopeful ideal took over in 1848 enough violence occurred to make their predecessors' fear of the lower classes seem more and more justifiable. The truth was, violence was present in society as a whole; only very few people were able to perceive this fact and to accept its implications. Karl Vogt, the biologist in the Frankfurt Assembly, saw beyond his contemporaries in this. When he asked himself whence came the brutality that attends every revolution, he noticed a phenomenon that is perennial:

"The brutality which is present in higher circles filters down, and this brutality which above lives only in thoughts, below takes the form of action. I have heard hundreds and hundreds of times expressions like 'The whole bunch ought to be knocked out with grape shot,' 'the agitators deserve to be hanged all together.' . . . Such expressions are mostly used by people who are fanatics of order and who make it their business to preach order and peace."

Vogt made this statement before the full force of the reaction had shown that when the upper classes had a chance to indulge themselves, in the interests of "restoring order," they were quite as capable of actual physical brutality as the men they feared.

A modern psychologist might speculate, where Vogt could not, that unconscious as well as conscious hatreds were bound to pervade any society held together with such rigid and arbitrary bonds as Europe in the mid-nineteenth century. The mass of the people were kept down not only by laws but by customs, by studied arrogance, by pious sanctions. Herzen quotes from a Russian writer who admired the west because everyone born there "learns in his cradle, in his games, in his mother's caresses, notions of duty, justice, law, and order." These are the very sources to which psychology today traces repressions. It may have been these same conceptions of duty, law, and order which had hogtied western Europe for centuries. Class hatred had persisted there from the Middle Ages; it is one of the most characteristic features of the twelfth century. What the nineteenth century failed to realize was that merely by overcoming people's conscious hostility, by trying sincerely to conciliate the classes, they could not also overcome the unconscious feelings that were bred into their bones. To speculate further, is it not reasonable to imagine that when new ideas loosened the sanctions which had kept each man in his place, a lot more force was let loose than men realized they had within them?

When hostility that has been repressed is first released into consciousness, there is a moment, for individuals at least, and perhaps also for nations, when it appears to be of uncontrollable violence. Perhaps this is because there exist, at first, no habitual or institutional skills for dealing with it overtly. Thus violence erupted among the lower classes as they began to dare to ask for more equal conditions, a violence which came in good part from the release of their old resentments. At the same time the upper classes, who were just beginning to dare to give more equality, found that this process simultaneously brought to the surface in themselves the fears which they had long kept hidden of the results of lower class resentment.

The great advantage which America had was that its social arrangements to a large measure prevented these hatreds from forming; not completely, but enough to make a startling contrast with Europe in those days.

Another psychological factor took the men of 1848 by surprise. It was noted by Massimo d'Azeglio, although its explanation had to wait for a hundred years — and that was the distinct ambivalence in the human soul toward freedom. It was not only the unexpected violence that shocked people, it was that freedom itself terrified them. This ambivalence has been expounded psychoanalytically by Erich Fromm, in *Escape from Freedom*. He shows that from the time of the Reformation freedom has been a burden, and indeed a threat, for men who are not prepared to accept its responsibilities — and there are many. This quality made every demand for a revolution two-faced, so that men were always retreating as well as moving forward, in spite of themselves. Or, as Massimo d'Azeglio perceived it: "The gift of liberty is like that of a horse, handsome, strong, and high-spirited. In some it arouses a wish to ride; in many others, on the contrary, it increases the desire to walk." A great many people felt more like walking as the year 1848 passed — all the French who voted for Napoleon, on the ground that he would restore "order," all the Prussians who paid their taxes after their parliament had been dissolved in the very act of telling the citizens not to pay them, all the Hapsburg subjects who in 1849 did not have a chance either to vote for anybody or to support a constitution. All these were people who found that the effort of doing something for themselves was not so rewarding as letting somebody on top do it — especially when it came to the task of overcoming the violence of the lower classes.

When the moderates took fright at the contemplation of their danger, they accused the radicals of trying to destroy order and property. To the radical intellectuals, this was ill-will and insult. They loved order and property and class conciliation as much as anybody, but being somewhat closer to the people than the other leaders they realized that they would not be satisfied with constitutions but would require some social reforms. None of the radicals had a chance to show how far he would go before he was stopped. He was lucky if he was stopped by foreign arms, as Mazzini was, so that his dream could go on. To be halted by civil war such as the June Days of Paris seemed to prove that the radical case was hopeless, or that, as Frederick William put it, soldiers are the only cure for democrats.

After the middle classes had won most of what they wanted, they often voluntarily gave up some of their new privileges so that the lower classes would not have to be given liberties too. They were like the man in the story who was asked what he would like best in the world, provided his worst enemy could have the same thing in double measure — and he answered, *one blind eye*. There was practically no one to say that the cure for democracy was more democracy.

This was the situation that Marx saw, and he thought of a brilliantly original answer. Do not minimize class conflict, exaggerate it. Even the most far-reaching concessions of the conciliators would not give workers an equal status in society, and the only way for them to achieve it would be to throw over all the privileged and property-clutching classes, ignoring the soft words of socialists like Louis Blanc as well as the turncoat policies of the Lamartines.

Thus when the 48ers failed they were beaten physically by the terrified conservatives, and also beaten intellectually by the theories of Marx, which made most socialist movements forget the poetical and discredited 1848 fancies.

To the men of 1848, class violence was anathema, but violence between nations was natural and often admirable. The French radical parties would have been as happy to march into Savoy or the Rhineland as the Germans were to march into Schleswig, or the Italians to chase Radetzky. Disarmament was preached only by eccentrics like Karl Vogt and, indeed, Louis Napoleon, neither of them typical of the 1848 spirit.

Marx branded nationality a myth, a verdict which was just as greatly opposed to 1848 ideas as was his doctrine of the class struggle; in fact the two went hand in hand. Loyalty to class, the Marxists maintained, would prevent international wars. But the men who wished to create nations realized that all classes must share in patriotism by having a stake in the nation, and the men who wanted peace between the classes felt that national loyalty was one way to encourage it. Thus the doctrines of struggle between classes and between nations were in inverse ratio. One may ask, of course, whether class is not a myth, whether property, at least the prestige that comes from property, is not a myth, whether ultimate democracy would not surmount all of these mythical obstacles. But the fact remains that the men who wanted democracy a hundred years ago planned to organize it in national units, and that political democracy has not yet succeeded in units any larger. These national blocs made plenty of trouble for the world, but perhaps no more than the class struggle.

The democratic spirit is elusive, and has first to be learned within a much smaller group even than a nation. It involves, first of all, a recognition in each man's soul that all other men are as good as he, at least potentially. Where could that spirit be born in Europe in 1848? Albert, the workingman, was called by his first name all the time he was a member of the French government; Baron Doblhoff in Vienna was suspected because he gave parties where the nobility could meet the middle classes socially for the first time; the King of Prussia could label an assembly of professors "the gutter"; Macaulay could stand up in the House of Commons to say that universal suffrage would destroy civilization and everything that made civilization worth while, the security of property; Sir Stratford Canning, Britain's ambassador to Turkey, could tear up Lamartine's proclamations with the remark that he would not live in a Europe run by reds and demagogues; Metternich doubted that society could exist along with freedom of the press; in Vienna an officer threw his shaving water out of the window, and the worker whom he drenched was arrested because he complained; Guizot was shocked that anyone could confound the welfare of the lower classes with that of society as a whole. In such a climate of opinion it is not strange

that even those men who had the ideal of democracy in their hearts found it was hard to explain to others, and almost as hard to live with themselves.

Democracy also involves the recognition in each man's soul that he is as good as other men, at least potentially. Donelson, the American consul at Berlin, believed that a republic could not succeed in Europe while thousands starved and millions lacked the sense of personal independence on which the American system rests. Cavour recognized the same point when he said that the lower classes in the New World would be shocked at the lack of dignity among European servants and workmen. Kossuth embarrassed his peasants when he addressed them with the plural or polite form of "you"; the Italian revolutionaries who pulled Count Hübner from his carriage did not assume the right to sit there in his place; in Italian the very word "democratic" came to mean shabby, so that one would speak of a democratic pair of shoes.

Could a common will emerge from such a society, an agreement of the sort that would guarantee more rights to the majority and would find the minority yielding gracefully? To build such a society the men of 1848 had the right start. With all the weight of custom and prejudice against them they labored to make a world where men would feel more equal, and to make nations within which this feeling could operate. Their mistake was that they miscalculated the barriers — even in their own souls. It was too easy for leaders of the people to become either mass hypnotists, like Held and Robert Blum, or authoritarian improvers. Mazzini, Louis Blanc and Kossuth were all democrats in theory but became autocratic when it came to putting their plans into action. Revelation, after being ousted from religion, as someone remarked at the time, had turned to politics, and every man thought he knew how to govern.

There were a few nuclei of real democratic spirit. Manin in Venice handled his affairs with more of it than any other 48er in power. In some of the guerrilla armies partial democracy worked, as in Garibaldi's, where a man might be a captain one day, a private the next. Democracy was in some of the workers' movements, such as the editorial board of *L'Atelier*, the French workers' paper, or in Born's club for workingmen in Berlin where he said, "We want a club in order to become men." It could be found in some of the universities, like the Aula at Vienna, and in other groups interested in progress such as the Italian scientific and agricultural congresses. It was from the development of such groups as these that democracy could eventually be born again in Europe.

The revolutions, then, seem like a hurling of violence against violence, the struggling of vast incompatibilities to be born together — the incompatibility of freedom for all with power for some; the incompatibility of class solidarity and national solidarity; the demands of race, of privilege, of recently born economic groups, and new intellectual groups to be heard amid all the din.

Yet when the people had a chance to express themselves quietly on these subjects they accomplished a good deal more toward a natural settlement of their troubles than did their leaders. The parliament of Prussia foreshadowed reforms that were still important and pressing for the Weimar republic, while the constitution of Kremsier solved the problems of administering territories of mixed populations better than the government of Vienna ever settled the question, and better than the Austrian or Hungarian or Croat rebels showed any signs of doing while they were in power. In fact, it was in these parliaments that the real creativity of the period lay, not in the short-lived improvisations of governments themselves provisional, nor yet in the spectacle of popular force which yet did not succeed in destroying the forces of reaction. The greatest failure of all in 1848 was that the men who had power never really trusted the people.

Was nothing gained by all the year of revolution, either from the violence or from the quiet talk? The answer is very little.

Some revolutions shake up society so that when the pieces fall together again they are in a new pattern which permits growth in a new direction. In 1848 that hardly happened. The Austrian serfs were freed, but did this make up for the extra repression on all other Austrian subjects? Italy made a new start toward greater freedom, but Germany was disillusioned about freedom. Some old illusions were destroyed, but the new myths created by men like Marx and Bismarck were as one-sided as the ones they supplanted and failed equally to represent a synthesis of values. The test of whether a revolution is successful is not whether some power with a new name exercises the same essential restraints as before (which happened in Europe in 1870), but whether some important group has won some important new freedom — economic, political, social, or religious.

Out of 1848 and its struggles no important new freedom was wrested. Instead men lost confidence in freedom and imagined they had made a great advance in sophistication by turning from idealism to cynicism. After 1848 classes and nations played power politics, each unashamed to get what it could each for itself with very little thought for the common welfare of society. This was not realism, though it was called *Realpolitik*. In 1870 this policy brought a new chance to win many of the specific demands of the 1848 revolutionaries, yet no one can say that the basic questions of justice and cooperation among classes and nations were settled at that time. For these problems failure was worse than mere failure, for no new chance arose. In 1914, at the time of the next continental explosion, many of the powers that had been half rotten in 1848 disappeared for good, but with them disappeared a good part of the class and nation structure itself. For the appeal of totalitarianism comes partly from its indifference to these problems which had seemed so unyielding to solution. Today millions of classless, stateless people crowd the continent in hatred and despair — and in a way they are the end product of the futility and ruthlessness of the 1848 revolutions.

CONCLUSION

FRANÇOIS FEJTÖ

In 1948 François Fejtö, a Hungarian writer who served for a time as his country's envoy to Paris, edited a historical symposium to commemorate the hundredth anniversary of the 1848 revolutions. The symposium was international in nature; fifteen historians of various nationalities contributed detailed analyses of the revolutionary movement as it manifested itself in their respective countries. In the volume's concluding chapter, reprinted below, Fejtö attempts to synthesize these differing national accounts and to determine if any consistent pattern can be found in the revolutionary events throughout Europe.

I think the people are magnificent.
Flaubert: "Education Sentimentale"

Hungary lies humbled at Your Majesty's feet" was the message sent by General Paskievich to Nicholas I after the capitulation at Világos. In the autumn of 1849 the tumult of the revolution had died down everywhere. Young Europe had been defeated. "Yes, we have been beaten and humiliated," Proudhon wrote some time afterwards in his *Confessions*. "We have all been scattered, imprisoned, disarmed and gagged. The fate of European democracy has slipped from our hands—from the hands of the people—into those of the Praetorian Guard." But this incorrigible revolutionary hastened to add: "But that does not make the war on Rome any more just and constitutional. Because Italy, Hungary and Poland protest in silence, it does not mean to say they have been struck off the list of nations. And we democratic socialists are still the party of the future."

Contemporary observers looked upon the bloody defeat of the liberal, democratic and nationalist movements of 1848 as an historical enigma. Contrary to all expectations, all hopes raised by the "people's spring," the Austrian, Russian and Prussian reactionaries had come out victorious. The French Republic, which had been born amidst so much bloodshed, became the springboard for a clever and unscrupulous adventurer. Nearly every state in Europe was under police control, informers flourished, and thousands of people were executed and imprisoned. Let us try to discover the reasons for this surprising setback.

John Stuart Mill seems to have hit the nail on the head in his study of the 1848 Revolution in France, when he points out that the bulk of the people were not prepared to accept the Revolution and take advantage of the rights offered them by the insurgents of Paris. This is even more true of the other peoples, for France had a higher cultural level and greater political experience than the rest of Europe. But even the French were incapable of making

From François Fejtö, "Conclusion," in *The Opening of an Era: 1848 — An Historical Symposium*, edited by François Fejtö with an introduction by A. J. P. Taylor (London, 1948), pp. 414–427. By permission of Allan Wingate (Publishers) Ltd.

full use of universal suffrage. Proudhon's prophecies and warnings were justified. In the first elections organised by the Republic, the republican candidates were in the minority, although contemporary observers unanimously declare that these elections were quite free and there was no interference by the authorities. The people simply would not back up their real friends. The republicans realised too late that it was impossible to improvise democracy, and that two months were not enough to make the whole country understand where they were aiming. "The people are not ready at all," Denis Poulot, the author of *Sublime,* said of the French. The German, Austrian and Hungarian peoples were even less ready, and throughout Europe middle-class and conservative elements formed the majorities in the new constituent assemblies. One can understand the genuine revolutionaries' despair at this unexpected set-back, and how their dissatisfaction with the elections resulted in the risings first at Rouen, then in Paris, Vienna and Budapest.

The political honesty of the French revolutionary leaders — due partly to their idealism and partly to their inexperience — also largely contributed to their defeat. These leaders were limited in what they could do, as they were members of coalition governments, whose opportunism paralysed their efforts. "Every collective (i.e. coalition) government is weak, hesitant and vacillating," wrote Lamartine in his *Histoire de la Révolution de 1848.* In addition to representatives of working-class interests, the French provisional Government included intellectuals and lower and upper-middle-class republicans. They neutralised one another and the Government's lack of harmony prevented it at the start from winning the confidence of the country, which the revolution had taken completely by surprise. It could only have gained the people's confidence by energetic measures and an unequivocal propaganda for the cause it stood for. Pillersdorf's Government in Austria and Batthyány's in Hungary were powerless for the same reason. The

only difference between the coalition governments formed in France and those of other European countries was that only in France were there representatives of working-class interests in the Government: Louis Blanc and Albert. All the various cabinets had failed, through indecision, to reform the machinery of the State, which went on functioning with its old personnel, in the old way.

We have seen that a large part of the middle class joined the revolutionaries not from their own inclinations but because they were driven to do so by the reactionaries. So it is not surprising that the middle-class element, in 1848 as in 1830, having been unable to prevent the revolution, did all it could to stop it as soon as possible. From the start, the middle and working classes had entirely different attitudes towards the revolution. The middle classes looked upon it as a means to strengthen their own authority and bring about the reforms which they considered to be immediately necessary. The people wanted something quite different and much more important: real equality and fraternity; in other words, a revised edition of the 1793 Revolution. The masses of Berlin, Vienna, Milan and Budapest all wanted social justice. But the idealists like Lamartine and Petöfi ran to help the middle classes in their distress. In France the conception of the Republic, and in Eastern Europe the conception of the Nation, were "the only means of escaping anarchy," as Lamartine said to the terrified deputies when the Chamber was being besieged by the people of Paris. Lamartine pointed out that anarchy would mean poverty, fanaticism and socialism. So when leaflets bearing the magic words: "The Republic has been proclaimed," were showered down on the mob demonstrating in the streets of Paris, eye-witnesses tell us that "a hundred thousand men raised their arms, and a single shout arose from the Place de la Grève . . ." The proclamation of a constitutional régime provoked the same enthusiasm in Turin, Berlin, Vienna, Pressburg and Budapest. But it very soon became clear that the words "Republic" and "Nation" had different meanings for the moderate and for the democrat, and, as Daniel Stern remarked, it became clear that "the middle class from reacting against the social revolution ended by reacting against the political one."

All the "united fronts," which had won the first victories of the revolution, broke up. Class interests soon appeared and prevailed over flowery speeches and political convictions. In every country, the revolutionaries were split into two camps: the "reds" who wanted to carry on the work they had begun to its ideological consequences, and the "blues" who wanted to prevent a social revolution. The two sides clashed in France on 22 June. Those bloody days, which were really caused by the workers' dissatisfaction with the middle-class republic and with exclusively political reforms, sealed the fate of the French Revolution and at the same time had a fatal influence on all the revolutions in Europe. The Czar Nicholas had every reason to rejoice at the catastrophic defeat of the workers in Paris, and to send Cavaignac his congratulations. The reactionaries alone profited by the conflict between the republican middle class and the workers. John Stuart Mill rightly pointed out that there was no cause for surprise in the middle-class National Guard's behaviour in the "Days of June." It had already hastened to help the regular army crush the democratic revolts of 1832 and 1834. It was its conduct in February 1848 which had been exceptional, when — to the amazement of Louis Philippe and his Government — it had caught the revolutionary fever.

Some weeks earlier, the British Government had shown how a revolution could be nipped in the bud. This time it was the republican Cavaignac's turn to prove that his vaunted Jacobinism was merely what Marx described as "the conservatism of the *juste milieu* disguised by a cloak of violence and an affectation of revolutionary spirit." His action greatly relieved all the moderates in the Government, who were perpetually

terrified of the people. It became plain that all those who had yielded to the pressure of the mob had been deluded: they had over-estimated the importance of the barricades. Engels, who was interested in the 1848–9 revolutions not only from a social but also a military point of view, later came to the conclusion that the barricades of 1848 had been primarily of a moral value.

After the June risings had been put down, the Governments of Central Europe set about dealing with their own popular movements with the serenity of men who have shaken off a nightmare. In his chapter on Austria, Doctor Endres mentions a fact which is far from being an isolated phenomenon: Schwarzer, the Minister for Public Works in the Vienna Government, actually provoked a revolt of the masses by lowering wages and making provocative declarations, so as to smash it with the support of public opinion. The reactionaries' reprisals were, in every country, all the more cruel, as they had been so terrified of what they called "terrorists" — a term under which they included not only Blanqui but men as mild as Cabet. The very existence of the National Workshops in France, and the public works undertaken in Austria to reduce unemployment, appeared to the middle class as violations of the sacred right of property. The French bill to nationalise the railways produced, despite its cautious phrasing, a storm of protest. The following lines, printed by Alexandre Dumas in his newspaper, sum up the middle class's attitude on the eve of the events in June: "The terrorists are out to destroy the country, the socialists are out to destroy the family, and the communists are out to destroy property." On 27 May the *Tribune Nationale* gave this picture of the state of the country: "The nation's finances are in chaos, law and order have been destroyed, everyone is in a state of ferment . . . justice is a matter of politics, ordinary civil rights have gone by the board . . . and all this is the doing of the Provisional Government." It is thought possible that these words may have been written by Baudelaire, who had been seen at the barricades in February. In June he looked upon the revolution as sheer folly. "The people are mad and the middle class is mad," he wrote in his diary.

Whilst the middle class was blinded by fear, the people were exasperated by the betrayal of their hopes. In the months following the revolution, class antagonism proved stronger than the ties of republicanism. The republican's lack of discipline (of which Proudhon, too, complained, looking upon it as one of the causes of defeat) assisted their opponents. Men like Louis Blanc and Ledru-Rollin considered that their most dangerous enemy was not the right wing, but Blanqui. Another reason for the left wing's weakness, was that instead of drawing up a definite programme, which would strengthen the Republic, they produced utopian proposals which they hoped would restore life to normal and calm the nation. Whilst the middle-class theorists wanted to bring in free trade at once, others (like Proudhon, whose proposals were accepted by Emile de Girardin) proclaimed the advantages of creating a "trade bank"; then there was Lamennais wanting the State to help the export trade. . . . This wave of theorising even engulfed the doctrinaires of the Republic, the staff of the *National,* who taking over the left wing's programme also recommended the formation of co-operative societies for production and distribution.

The romantic and unrealistic character of the February Revolution is of course explained by the fact that the working class had asserted itself for the first time, and that its hopes could not be fulfilled even if all the middle-class demands, however radical, were satisfied. The middle class merely wanted political democracy, but the workers also wanted work and food. Marx was the first to point out that revolutionary excesses of highly developed peoples have a disturbing influence on the reformist movements of backward ones. Events in Germany might very well have taken an entirely different turn if the German middle classes had not caught the fear of the workers, of revolution — and above all — of communism. According to Marx, "their own revolutionary ardour was considerably cooled." Influenced by the working-class movements in France and, to some extent, in England, the middle classes of more backward countries, although in actual fact they had less reason than their opposite numbers in the west to fear their own proletariat or communism, became political reactionaries before they had completed their historical mission as progressives. Consequently, whilst on the one hand the very fact of the February Revolution breaking out had a stimulating effect on revolutionary movements in either action or preparation, on the other, the social conflicts which were wrecking the French revolutionary movement had the opposite effect of breaking up the united fronts of the various classes and parties representing the forces of progress.

The *volte-face* of an important section of the middle class was probably made easier by the fact that towards the middle of 1848 it was plain that the economic crisis had reached its climax — at any rate in Britain, where it started. The middle class regained confidence in its own economic system and it patiently waited for the end of the revolution and the restoration of law and order. The middle-class citizens of Paris, looking out of their windows on the streets seething with people as though there were a perpetual holiday, thought that the country had gone mad. George Sand, whose extremist articles had done a good deal to scare the middle class, writes in her memoirs: "There is the sound of a drum and the cries of the newsvendors . . . the *garde mobile* goes by . . . a tree of liberty is planted . . . then there are the delegations, the ceremonies, the bands of priests and soldiers and Poles and Italians." Such a spectacle daily strengthened the middle-class Parisians' desire to see the return of law and order. "We must put a stop to it," they were all saying. This desire for social discipline caused a *rapprochement* between the middle-class moderates, both in Paris and other European capitals, with the conservatives and reactionaries; and finally — in Prussia, Austria, Poland and Hungary — with the very government circles they had all been fighting on the eve of the Revolution.

But the revolutions of 1848 did not fail solely because the economic crisis which had helped precipitate them was neither deep-rooted nor lasting, or because the middle class, which appeared to be destined to control these revolutions and consolidate the ground won, deserted them out of fear of the working class. International politics also contributed to the disaster of 1848. Despite the apparent unanimity of these revolutions, which broke out almost simultaneously, they were not co-ordinated. The revolutionaries' solidarity — with rare exceptions like the October Revolution in Vienna — was shown only in proclamations made by the various revolutionary governments and parliaments, which sent each other messages of sympathy. And from the spring of 1848 onward, it came out that the newly awakened national feelings were much harder to conciliate than some of the fanatical exponents of the new doctrines had imagined. Marx and Engels, the editors of the *Neue Rheinische Zeitung*, later on severely criticised Michael Bakunin for saying in his *Appeal to the Slavs*, on the occasion of the pan-Slav Congress of Prague, that he hoped that democratic nationalism would bring peace and freedom to all the people, without exception.

The attitude of the founders of socialism towards racial problems, and especially pan-Slavism, is worth consideration.

The contributors to this book almost unanimously agree that the decline of nationalism into chauvinism was mainly due to the middle-class attempt to solve internal problems by creating antagonism between the different nations. Mazzini gives an excellent analysis of Charles Albert's dilemma over the revolution, in his *Republic and Monarchy in Italy*. The King of Piedmont, he pointed out, was frightened of losing his throne if he were defeated, but he was also afraid of the liberties which the people would demand after fighting for him. Carlo Cattaneo's comment on Charles Albert (in his Memoirs published in 1849) was: "He is at war to prevent the proclamation of a Republic in Milan." The unsolved social problems were a major reason why the Hungarian Revolution, one of the most important liberal movements of 1848, degenerated into a racial conflict. Proudhon criticised the liberals among the minor nobility in Hungary for refusing to grant the Slavs and Rumanians within their borders the same national rights that they were so bravely defending against the centralising policy of Vienna. This petty aristocracy claimed that these races were as backward compared with the Hungarian ruling class as the Bretons, Normans and Catalans were by comparison with the French. Marx and Engels, on the other hand, supported the Hungarians' point of view. This was not, however, because they felt any particular sympathy for the Hungarians, or even — as some of their enemies said — out of an unconscious spirit of German imperialism. Marx and Engels clearly showed by their attitude towards the Polish problem that they were capable of subordinating German interests to the wider ones of Europe. But they were convinced that Europe's progress was best served by the great civilised nations such as the Italians, the Germans, the Poles and the Hungarians. As for the small Slav nations — such as the Czechs and the Serbs — Marx and Engels considered that they could not help but be counter-revolutionaries. They believed that the Serbs, the Croats, the Czechs and the Slovaks were historically bound to disappear, becoming part of their more civilised neighbours. Their geographical and economic conditions were such that they could not remain independent nations, and that even their sincerest democrats, once they wished their people to form a nation, were forced to become counter-revolutionaries and the tools of reaction. The real Slav

Congress, wrote Marx and Engels, was not the one Windischgrätz's artillery blew to pieces in Prague, but the Austrian Army itself, mainly composed of Slavs, which easily liquidated the democrats of Bohemia and — with rather more difficulty — the patriots of Hungary.

Marx and Engels had no use for the sentimentalists who bewailed the fate of small nations, which, they said, had to give way to the superior needs of the big nations. If the Slavs were to realise their dream of a great Southern Slav State, Hungary, Austria and Germany would lose the outlet they needed on the Adriatic. The founders of scientific socialism quoted the example of the war between the United States and Mexico. The American middle class had annexed Texas, yet who would dream, they asked, of weeping for that country's lost independence? Marx and Engels were so certain that the interests of the small Slav nations clashed with those of the proletariat, that they were not prepared to take the Czechs' and Croats' desire for independence seriously. And they considered that Bakunin's pan-Slavism was directed, whether or not he intended it, against the revolutionary elements in the Austrian Empire, and was therefore "reactionary from the start and by its very nature."

Marx and Engels were to maintain this attitude for several decades, and it was only round about the 'eighties that their followers corrected it. In the light of recent events, it would seem that Bakunin was right. He had defended not only the idea of a federation of all the republics in Europe, but he had also predicted that the small Slav nations would play an important part in this vast federation. Like most of their democratic contemporaries, Marx and Engels were dazzled by the heroism of the Hungarian people, by the manufacture of arms in the national workshops, by the introduction of paper money, by the judgments of the revolutionary tribunals, and by that "permanent revolution" which recalled the triumphs of the Great Revolu-

tion in France. But the Hungarian nobles' strict liberalism came too late in 1848, particularly as — even when Hungary's very existence as a nation was in danger — they refused to grant the lower classes (whether or not they spoke Hungarian) truly equal rights and the complete abolition of serfdom.

So 1848 was not only the spring of living peoples, but also — in the words of the great Rumanian patriot Barnutin — the time of "the resurrection of dead races." But these races — the Rumanians, the Southern Slavs and the Slovaks — were dead only politically speaking: they had retained their own languages and culture throughout centuries of oppression. The truth of George Sand's axiom — "nations can do nothing if they are isolated" — is clearly shown by the manner in which Austria made use of the tragic antagonisms between the different races comprising the Empire. After 1848, all the forces which were to lead to the disintegration of the Austro-Hungarian Empire and the creation of Yugoslavia, Czechoslovakia and Rumania, were very much in evidence. The proposals to create these States were first put forward by Slav theorists at the time of the Revolution. Kossuth, during his exile in Turin in 1862, when he was meditating on his own revolutionary experience, conceived the idea of a free confederation of all the Danubian peoples: Hungary, Transylvania, Rumania, Croatia and Serbia. He envisaged this free confederation as he realised that it would be impossible to create a centralised State in the area between the Carpathians, the Adriatic and the Black Sea. He wrote in a Turin paper:

It would be no use for a Danubian nation to annex its neighbours' territory; so long as it remained isolated, it would be in danger, and it would fall in the end to a foreign Power. The Magyars, the Yugoslavs and Rumanians must unite and form a Danubian Confederation. Then they will form a first-class power: a rich and powerful State of thirty million inhabitants, with weight in Europe. I honestly and wholeheartedly recommend union, peace and friendship between the Magyars, the Rumanians and the Slavs, as their one means of assuring a successful future.

The "united front" of the nations in revolt against European absolutism in 1848 was just as weak as the internal conditions of the progressives within each nation. The revolutionary parliaments and Governments all failed in their duty towards the liberal and democratic sections of the people. Only the extreme left wings, which formed a tiny but powerful minority, fought to the end for brotherhood between the nations. The history of French politics at the time shows the great gulf between the revolutionary Government's theory and its practice. Lamartine's foreign policy differed from Guizot's only in the tone of its announcements, for he was primarily concerned with avoiding a war. It is certain that if France had given her full support to the revolutionary movements in Europe — from Italy to Belgium and from Belgium to Ireland — she would have been involved in a war with Britain. The majority of members of the Provisional Government dared not take the responsibility. And yet the left wing middle-class leaders also wanted to relax the tension within France by undertaking a foreign war.

Henri Martin, in his book on Manin, the leader of the Venetian revolt, strongly criticises the revolutionary Government's noninterventionist policy, which left the Venetians isolated, in impotent rage. Martin was convinced that if the great demonstration in May had taken place on the banks of the Adige instead of the Seine, there would have been no working-class revolts in June. The British Ambassador, Lord Normanby, also thought that the French Republic would be forced to declare war to solve her own problems. The Second Republic's domestic difficulties resulted — even without a war — in Bonapartism. But the real reason for its collapse was neither its failure to declare war nor its inability to resolve social conflicts by a *coup d'état*: it was its middle-class leaders' lack of experience, initiative

and cool-headedness. They had not sufficient confidence in themselves to break down all opposition, and smash all the conspiracies, for they had not yet accepted their own creation, the Republic, as the best form of government.

So France left the other revolutionary movements in Europe — particularly those of Venice and Hungary — to their fate, and they accused her of denying her ideals. One wonders, nevertheless, if anyone would have believed in the honesty of France's intentions if she had given military aid to Italy. Palmerston would not have been alone in his suspicions: the Italians themselves were almost as frightened of French intervention as the Austrians. And what about the Germans? Had the Frankfort Assembly really proved its solidarity and political sense by applauding Welcker's plea for "our brothers in captivity in Alsace"? The few extreme left-wing pronouncements in favour of the Poles or the Italians were received in stony silence. Under the majority of the German deputies' liberal phraseology it was not hard to discover their conviction that, as Bismarck put it in 1850, "the basic principle of a great State is not a romantic attitude but political enigma." The Pressburg Diet had not shown any higher political morality, when it lacked the courage openly to refuse the Viennese Court's demand for reinforcements for the Austro-Hungarian army fighting in Italy. The majority of revolutionary leaders pursued a traditional foreign policy, which helped to undermine the success of their domestic policy. The middle class succeeded in making the foreign policy of the old order that had been destroyed acceptable to the masses: dynastic egoism became national egoism. Thus were the seeds sown of what was to become, if not a determining factor of the 1871 war and the great wars of the twentieth century, at any rate the pretext for them.

The mistakes made by the masses and immature classes of society greatly facilitated the work of the British and Russian statesmen, who had tried from the start of the revolution to localise the movement and maintain the balance of power in Europe.

I have already said of Great Britain that her very existence, her highly developed social structure and her interior conflicts stimulated the reformists. From that point of view Britain may be said to have been one of the chief agents of the revolution. But one might also fairly say that her very existence as so powerful a country that France dared not oppose her, prevented the revolution from spreading. Britain, under Palmerston, cannot strictly be called reactionary, as her foreign policy was based on the defence of moderate reformist tendencies, but when the choice lay between the revolution and the restoration of the reactionary *status quo*, Britain chose (though admittedly not without some hesitation) the second alternative. Although the reconstitution of a reactionary Europe was not in Britain's commercial interests, it would not, like the revolution, threaten the very existence of the British Empire. Hawkins, the British Consul in Venice, was himself a Tory, but he was undoubtedly expressing the view of the whole of the British ruling class when he said to Manin that if Britain were to admit the justice of the Lombards' claims, she would be in no position to deny the demands for independence of her subjects in India, Ireland, the Ionian Islands and, generally speaking, in all her colonies. So Britain's paradoxical position was that on the one hand she had contributed to the outbreak of the revolutions, and on the other she did all she could to halt their progress and ensure the victory of the reactionaries.

As for the second Great Power, Russia, her attitude towards the democratic movements was clear from the start. Nicholas I had advised the Courts of both Prussia and Austria to crush the revolutionaries, encouraging them in their belief that — as Frederick William IV wrote to Bunsen — "the only way to deal with democrats is by force of arms." It was on the Czar's advice that Robert Blum, the Viennese representative in the Frankfort Parliament (who,

after being involved in the October Revolution, fell into Windischgrätz's hands) was condemned to death and executed. By occupying the Danubian provinces and Transylvania, and later by attacking Hungary in 1849, Czarist Russia had followed the traditions of the Holy Alliance, but she had also — according to Palmerston — acted against her own imperial interests, as she had helped to save her rival, Austria.

The experiences of 1848 thus showed once again that political and social reform in modern Europe was not each nation's private affair, but had international repercussions, especially amongst the Great Powers. Henceforth, Austria and Turkey remained in existence not by virtue of their own Governments' strength, but because the Great Powers considered that their continuation was "in the public interest." It was symbolical that the great Austrian Empire had to be assisted by another vast Empire before she could quell the revolution in the little State of Hungary. The close connection between domestic and foreign policy was evident in the widespread opinion that the ideas of freedom and democracy were simply accessories of French propaganda. Britain might have fought with less spirit against the democrats of Europe had she not looked upon them as virtual allies of France. There can be no doubt that the main reason why the 1848 revolutions failed was because of the hostility of the two great European powers which intervened to smash them: Britain by financial and diplomatic means, and Russia by force of arms.

In the autumn of 1849 Europe was much less free than she had been in the spring of 1848. People at the time wondered in their disillusionment what had been the use of the popular risings which had taken place practically everywhere in Europe. Might it not have been better if social and political advances had come gradually, without violent upheavals, simply as the result of the technical, economic and intellectual forces that were so busily at work?

Put like that, the question seems absurd. It presupposes that the leaders and the masses had a far more direct effect on events than they had: as Ledru-Rollin pointed out, they followed rather than led the way. Instead of querying the value of revolutions, it is more sensible to try and discover why they should be necessary. They are cataclysms whose value and significance lies not in their accelerating evolution, but in the fact that they result from the clash between the dynamic force of progress and the static strength of conservatism. Revolutions, like the great tragedies, lift for a moment the veil hiding "humanity's secret." This secret is the passionate spirit of the people who appear on the stage of history only when the world is experiencing the birth-pangs of a new phase in its development. Machiavelli, in his *Meditations on Livy*, heavily underlines the need for nations, if they are not to degenerate, to return from time to time to their basic moral principles. Revolutions are justified by the fact that they do return to them.

Eighteen forty-eight in the history of Europe and the world, marks the spread of new ideas and new aims, which thenceforth became common property. If we look at the revolution from the point of view of its ideas and aims, we can say that the reactionaries only appeared to be the victors in 1848 and 1849. Engels and Proudhon almost simultaneously realised that "the gravediggers of the 1848 revolutions became their executors." The Chartists were laughed at and the German and French socialists and communists persecuted, but the British House of Commons voted laws to protect the workers which Marx hailed as the first legislation enshrining socialist principles. And under the Second Empire, in spite of the despotic behaviour of the authorities, the working-class movement continued to grow, remaining faithful to the principles of its heroes, now in their graves, in exile or in prison. The movements in Vienna and Hungary were also crushed, but their chief accomplishment, the abolition of serfdom, remained. And an extraordinary thing was that the reactionary Austrian Governments that came to power after the revolution completed the modernisation (in the middle-class sense of the word) of the executive, thereby fulfilling one of the main tasks that the revolutionaries had set themselves.

The French elections in April and December 1848, and later the result of the plebiscite, did not finally shake the democrats' faith in the people and the universal suffrage they had wanted it to possess. On the contrary, during the next hundred years, the peoples' battle for the extension of the franchise was to take a major place in the history of European politics. The February Revolution, as John Stuart Mill noted, opened new vistas for the people, on the day on which universal suffrage was proclaimed law. The 1848 Revolution clearly showed that the extension of the right to vote and the democrats' efforts to bring about the political emancipation of the ever-growing masses, was no "middle-class affair," but a foretaste of the political institutions of the future. The capitalist middle class was not democratic — it was at the most liberal — at the beginning of its struggle for power. Whenever possible, it did its utmost to prevent the introduction of universal suffrage and all the economic, political and educational reforms demanded by the equalitarians. This should not surprise us, for it is in the middle class's vital interest to preserve its economic privileges and the political and legal advantages which guarantee them.

Democracy was connected with the capitalist upper-middle class only in so far as it drove the masses toward an ideology which served the interests of the lower-middle class, the peasants, the intellectuals and the factory workers, none of whom had the advantages of possessing capital. Although the middle class succeeded, in the countries in which it had gained social, economic and political control, in making a caricature of democratic aims, by preventing the social consequences of political equality, that does not mean to say that democracy was closely linked to the future of capitalism and the middle class. The upper-middle class of every country in 1848 showed that it had more important prizes to win than democracy. But the Revolution did bring about an alliance between the social reformers and the democrats, between "the thinkers and the oppressed"; and that alliance was to become in the course of the next century, a major historical factor.

But the "gravediggers" of the revolution who became its "executors" were principally concerned with carrying out the national clauses in its will. Neither Radetzky nor Schwarzenberg nor Nicholas I could stand in the way of German and Italian unity. Engels, looking back on the events of 1848 a quarter of a century afterwards, remarked that "with the exception of Poland, the great European nations had won independence and unity." There remained the small nations in Europe and elsewhere. For the past hundred years, the ideas of independence abroad in 1848 have never ceased revolutionising the world; they have affected every race, starting with the white and going on to the coloured peoples, and they have threatened all the old empires and prevented any attempt to create new ones.

Socialism, democracy, nationalism in its best sense, and internationalism in the sense of a recognition of the nations' interdependence: those were the predominant themes of the revolutions of 1848. Like all revolutions, they marked both a beginning and an end. Daniel Stern, one of its most interesting historians, defined the revolution as "the final collapse of the old alliance between the Catholic Church and the monarchies, and the disappearance of the last trace of the 'Divine Right of Kings' . . ." that was the political victory of the 1848 Revolution, which the educated classes won in the name of Liberty. The first attempt to set up modern government, the foundation of rational, republican unity won by the working classes in the name of Equality and Fraternity — that was its social victory. This double character of the 1848 Revolu-

tion, political and social, due to the fact that the interests of the middle class both combined and clashed with those of the working class, caused its essential contradiction. Sometimes it seemed that it had taken place too late and sometimes — as in the case of the proletarian risings and the revolts of the small nations in central Europe — that it had broken out too soon.

The 1848 Revolution was the work of Young Europe: young races, young social classes and young men. The students played a valiant part, and they formed the vanguard of the movement in Paris, Dresden, Vienna, Budapest, Transylvania and the Serbian provinces. That is why there were so many utopian dreams and so much lyrical enthusiasm. The poets, from Lamartine to Petöfi, were in the heart of the battle. Flaubert makes Frédéric Moreau, the hero of *Education Sentimentale*, reel through the streets of Paris in a state of exaltation, "as though the heart of all mankind beat in his breast." There were Frédérics in every city in Europe: they were the real heroes of 1848, fighting at the barricades, heedless of their personal safety, applauding the abolition of the death penalty — and demanding the guillotine for the enemies of the Republic.

The most dangerous delusion of the 1848 Revolution was what Proudhon called "republican mysticism": the belief that by the very fact of its existence, the Republic would produce social harmony and peaceful progress. The "Days of June" betrayed the illusion of social harmony. The bitterness of the conflict between the workers and the middle class was a shock from which the "Frédérics" never recovered, for their sacrifices had been made purely so as to effect a reconciliation between the two classes.

The discovery of their irreconcilable antagonism made 1848 a turning-point in modern history. Some never got over their disillusionment, and they were the ones whose bitterness created the "realist" school of literature and said with Flaubert's young hero that the time had come to be positive.

Others, such as the exponents of historical materialism, noted with satisfaction that the events of June justified their theories and taught the professional revolutionaries the necessity of dispensing with illusion, facing facts and continuing to work for social freedom in full knowledge of the long distance they had to travel, and the number of obstacles in their path.

After 1848 the revolutionaries grew tougher, and their naïve optimism gave place to a better understanding of the psychology of the masses.

The failure of the revolutions had a profound influence on European thought, and gave a fresh impulse to the study of historical philosophy and economics. This renascence alone made the 1848 Revolution a period of fertile experience. It seems as though history decided that the tragic themes of the dramas to be enacted in the centuries to come should be summed up in one great prologue. The hero of these dramas was to be, in the words of Baudelaire, "Mankind in search of happiness."

SUGGESTIONS FOR ADDITIONAL READING

Many participants and contemporaries have left accounts of the revolutionary events of 1848. Outstanding among these are *The Recollections of Alexis de Tocqueville* (edited by J. P. Mayer, London, 1948), one of the most astute and perceptive political observers of mid-nineteenth century France. Alphonse de Lamartine, the Romantic poet who headed the Provisional Government after the overthrow of Louis-Philippe, wrote a two-volume justification of his role in his *History of the French Revolution of 1848* (Boston, 1852), and Carl Schurz, who became a famous American statesman after he fled his native Germany following the defeat of the revolution there, gives a stirring picture of the youthful hopes raised by the outbreak of the revolution in his *Reminiscences* (Volume I, Chapter V–VII, New York, 1913).

Because of the later importance of the Communist movement, Karl Marx's diatribes on the 1848 revolutions have received close attention. The series of articles appearing under his name in the *New York Tribune* during 1851 and 1852 were actually written by Friedrich Engels, and they have been gathered together in book-form under the title *Revolution and Counter-Revolution, or Germany in 1848* (Chicago, 1914). Marx's interpretation of the events in France in 1848 is contained in *The Class Struggles in France* (New York, 1924) and in his brilliantly written monograph *The Eighteenth Brumaire of Louis Bonaparte* (Chicago, 1914).

Documents dealing with the revolutionary movements of 1848 in the various countries are to be found in Chapter IV of *Revolution from 1789 to 1906*, edited by R. W. Postgate (London, 1920). He has also written an entertaining account of the events from January 1 to December 31 of 1848 in his *Story of a Year: 1848* (New York, 1956). Other lively and somewhat journalistic accounts are to be found in J. Eastwood and P. Tabori, *'48, The Year of Revolutions* (London, 1948) and G.

Woodcock, *A Hundred Years of Revolution: 1848 and After* (London, 1948).

Most important of the scholarly attempts to deal with 1848 is the symposium, edited by François Fejtö, *The Opening of an Era: 1848* (London, 1948) to which leading scholars have contributed excellent articles. Arnold Whitridge in his *Men in Crisis: The Revolutions of 1848* (New York, 1949) surveys the revolutions from the standpoint of some of the leading personalities involved, while Priscilla Robertson emphasizes the social aspects in her *Revolutions of 1848: A Social History* (Princeton, 1952). The most brilliant analysis of the political problems is to be found in Sir Lewis B. Namier's *1848: The Revolution of the Intellectuals* (London, 1945).

Turning from the general European scene to individual countries, there are a number of fine monographs and studies. The revolution in France is treated in chapters V and VI of G. Lowes Dickinson's classic work *Revolution and Reaction in Modern France* (2nd ed., London, 1938); chapters V and VI of E. L. Woodward's *French Revolutions* (London, 1934); and chapter IV of John Plamenatz, *The Revolutionary Movement in France, 1815–1871* (London, 1952). Economic aspects are dealt with most fully in J. Marriott, *The French Revolution of 1848 in Its Economic Aspect* (2 vols., Oxford, 1913) and in Donald C. McKay's excellent study, *The National Workshops: A Study in the French Revolution of 1848* (Cambridge, Mass., 1933).

For Germany, there is still much merit in J. G. Legge's entertaining work, *Rhyme and Revolution in Germany; A Study in German History, Life, Literature and Character, 1813–1850* (London, 1918). In contrast to Namier's trenchant criticism of the Frankfurt Assembly, there is Veit Valentin's monumental work which has been abridged and translated as *1848: Chapters in German History* (London, 1940).

G. M. Trevelyan has written two classics

on the Italian phase of the revolutionary movement: *Garibaldi's Defense of the Roman Republic, 1848–1849* (London, 1907, 1949) and *Manin and the Venetian Revolution of 1848* (London, 1923). An extremely detailed account is provided in the three volumes of G. F. H. and J. Berkeley, *Italy in the Making, 1815–1848* (Cambridge, England, 1932–1940). The background of some elements of the Italian revolt is skilfully set forth by Kent R. Greenfield in *Economics and Liberalism in the Risorgimento: A Study in Nationalism in Lombardy,* 1814–1848 (Baltimore, 1934), and the international aspects of the revolution are set forth in A. J. P. Taylor, *The Italian Problem in European Diplomacy, 1847–1849* (Manchester, 1934). Gaetano Salvemini's illuminating study of *Mazzini* has recently been translated into English (Stanford, 1957).

The older work of C. Edmund Maurice, *The Revolutionary Movement of 1848–9 in Italy, Austria-Hungary, and Germany* (New York, 1887) is still useful, although it has been largely superseded by more modern studies of events in Central Europe. Foremost among these is R. John Rath, *The Viennese Revolution of 1848* (Austin, Texas, 1957). Also important are Jerome Blum, *Noble Landowners and Agriculture in Austria, 1815–1848: A Study in the Origins of the Peasant Emancipation of 1848* (Baltimore, 1948) and Adolph Schwarzenberg, *Prince Felix zu Schwarzenberg, Prime Minister of Austria, 1848–1852* (New York, 1926).

To the student who wishes to investigate the events of 1848 primarily from the standpoint of the ideologies involved, only a sampling of the voluminous writings can be mentioned here. For doctrines of liberalism the basic work remains Guido de Ruggiero, *The History of European Liberalism* (London, 1927) with its comparisons of English, French, German, and Italian varieties of liberalism. Benedetto Croce, *History of Europe in the Nineteenth Century* (New York, 1933) is primarily concerned with the concept of liberty as it developed during that period. For nationalism, there are C. J. H. Hayes, *Essays on Nationalism* (New York, 1926) and *The Historical Evolution of Modern Nationalism* (New York, 1931, 1948); Hans Kohn, *Prophets and Peoples: Studies in Nineteenth Century Nationalism* (New York, 1946); Louis L. Snyder, *The Meaning of Nationalism* (New Brunswick, N. J., 1954); and Boyd C. Shafer, *Nationalism: Myth and Reality* (New York, 1955). Doctrines and practices of conservatism are discussed in E. L. Woodward, *Three Studies in European Conservatism: Metternich, Guizot, the Catholic Church in the Nineteenth Century* (London, 1929) and Peter Viereck, *Conservatism Revisited: The Revolt Against Revolt, 1815–1949* (New York, 1949). Books on socialism abound, and the student will find a good introduction to the subject in Alexander Gray, *The Socialist Tradition: Moses to Lenin* (London, 1946); Edmund Wilson, *To the Finland Station: A Study in the Writing and Acting of History* (New York, 1940); and Volume I of *Socialism and American Life* (Princeton, 1952), edited by Donald Drew Egbert and Stow Persons.

Those students who are especially interested in American history can trace some of the impact of European events on our own country in Arthur J. May, *Contemporary American Opinion of Mid-Century Revolutions* (Philadelphia, 1927) and A. E. Zucker, editor, *The Forty-Eighters: Political Refugees of the German Revolution of 1848* (New York, 1950).

Finally, there are several historiographical articles which review the literature on various aspects of 1848 and which can guide the student to more detailed works: Paul Farmer, "Some Frenchmen Review 1848," *Journal of Modern History,* Vol. XX, No. 4 (December, 1948), pp. 320–325; John A. Hawgood, "The Frankfurt Parliament of 1848–49," *History,* Vol. XVII (July, 1932), pp. 147–151; and Theodore S. Hamerow, "History and the German Revolution of 1848," *American Historical Review,* Vol. LX, No. 1 (October, 1954), pp. 27–44.